PRAISE FOR <u>INSPIRED BY THE HOLY SPIRIT</u>

An amazing God-gifted writer, Georgie has the unique ability to express the deep emotions of her heart, touching the hearts of her readers in a profound and personal way. You will need a handkerchief before you are done.

Pastor Becky Vos

Georgie's words really touched me. I could feel her pain and her joy. These are profoundly moving stories that touch the soul.

Sharon Teal Coray, Artist

The stories in this book have touched my soul and mirrored the same thoughts I have lived.

Shirley Miller, Friend

"Inspired by the Holy Spirit" is a light in the darkness and encouragement for the weary soul.

Jan Erickson, Businesswoman and Writer

I have lived over three quarters of a century and am a Christian. I've never read any spiritual stories that could compare to the writings of Georgie Linnebur.

Ace Avery, Realtor and Published Poet

COPYRIGHT PAGE

DEDICATION

This book is dedicated first of all, to the Holy Spirit, who was my guide in writing these stories.

Secondly, I dedicate it to my mother, Mercedes Rosario Zdunowski. Besides being my mother, she was my best friend in life. We were inseparable. No matter how far I travelled, nothing stopped her from being with me. She was my great encourager to compile these stories and write this book.

ACKNOWLEDGEMENTS

I want to thank all those who helped and contributed towards the making of this book, including:

My son and artist, Chris A. Linnebur

Artist, Sharon Teal Coray

Editor, Becky Vos

Publisher, Sally Beesley

And my many friends and family who have encouraged and anticipated the completion of my first book, Inspired by the Holy Spirit.

Contents

INSPIRED BY THE HOLY SPIRIT

The Lord Will Never Leave You

PREFACE

This book has been in the works for the past twenty plus years of my life.

Some of these stories will remind you of your own happy times with your family, childhood memories of carefree days growing up, and cherished moments of profound love and companionship. Many others will testify to you of the common truth that, even when going through deep and dark trials, there is victory. God is always there for you, even in the blackest hours.

My hope is that as you read these stories you will realize you have access to the God of the Universe, to help you in anything. He loves you with unfathomable compassion and power. The Lord has ALWAYS been there throughout my lifetime, to encourage and protect me. He never left my side. He has talked with me and shown me stories about the light and dark I experienced, giving me amazing insights into His spiritual kingdom. Writing what He told me has helped to lighten my burdens and heal my soul.

May you sense His presence as you read my gift from God and now my gift to you, these stories, Inspired by the Holy Spirit.

TWO HEARTS JOINED TOGETHER AS ONE

"Therefore shall a man leave his father and his mother, and shall cleave unto his wife: and they shall be one flesh."

Genesis 2:24

Pop and Mami on Wedding Day, August 1945

JUST AS MANY STEPS

It all started with the words, "There are just as many steps from me to you, as there are from you to me." One year later, it ended with, "I do".

Many years before the steps, there was a beautiful island pearl. She was a strong spirit and character, very independent. As a mere child of seven years old, she took walks through the streets of Old San Juan, ending up at the old fortress, El Morro, often joining the fishermen while waiting for her father's return from the sea. Her father was a sailor on the

Liberty Ships, travelling far and near. He was a brave and smart man with so many talents. When at last they saw each other, he would hug her tight, then lift her up on to his shoulders, walking home that way. She would sing to him one of her favorite songs, "I want to be a sailor, sailing off to sea".

Far to the north of Puerto Rico, in the United States in the small town of Reading, Pennsylvania, lived a boy of seven years who was known as the leader of The River Rats. With this group of boys, he would traverse the sewer pipes near his home on a makeshift boat, along with his trusty 22 rifle. He was a sharpshooter at a young age and did not miss his target very often. Keep in mind the rats in the sewer were as big as a housecat or a small dog. He and his boys would kill the river rats coming out of the sewer at the Schuylkill River. He was a "Huckleberry Finn" with many wonderful dreams and plans.

Fast forward to the year 1945 when both these precious people are brought together by the Lord's hand. The course of their lives was to be forever changed - our Paradise Island Pearl and the King River Rat.

Mami was working for the USO in San Juan, selling war bonds. Pappa was lying on a bench next to the ocean waiting for a bus.

Mami came out of the USO Center to catch her bus and she caught her first glimpse of Pappa. Her first impression of him was – look at that poor American soldier -- what a shame. Pappa had had a few too many beers at the USO Club. Mami just walked away and headed towards the bus stop. Pappa staggered slowly to the same bus stop. Mami and her friend, Anna Lou, were going to the university. Mami looked at him, and said, "Are you ok?" He responded, "I am fine". Then Mami responded, "Why don't you go back to the base?" But instead of answering that question, Pappa gave Mami a quick kiss and walked away.

A year later, Mami was living in a different town, Ponce, Puerto Rico. One day Mami and Aunt Carmella were sitting at the large, circular water fountain at the middle of the Plaza. Surprise, surprise! Pappa was one of the soldiers at the Plaza that day too. The army had transferred him from San Juan to Ponce. He did not notice her at first, but when he did, he called to her, "Come over here". Mami responded, "The same steps that are from here to there are also from there to here." They compromised and met each other half-way. After some conversation, Pappa walked Mami home and met Grandmom, waiting at the door. She asked Mami, "Where are you going with that soldier?" "I invited him to join us for supper". Every Sunday Grandmom cooked for soldiers. It was a family tradition practiced since the Spanish-American War.

After that first Sunday dinner together with the family, Mami and Pappa had many more encounters. Going to the movies became a common adventure for them. Cowboy movies for Pappa, and tear-jerkers for Mami; they loved them all. Pappa dreamed of his horse ranch and Mami of her dream house. Sometimes Grandmom would go along, or another family member or close family friend. It was normal and proper back then to have a chaperone go with you on dates.

Besides going to the picture shows, they loved to dance. The Jitterbug was the "in" dance craze. Mami always loved to sing and dance. She was perfection at any type of dancing. Pappa was a fantastic dancer too. Fast beat, or slow dancing, he loved it all. What a rich combination they were. It was like Fred and Ginger on the dance floor, gliding with elegance, never missing a beat. They also loved to take long walks. Going to the beach was breathtaking. Just walking next to the Caribbean Sea along the sandy beach was so inspiring. The island itself was so magical; the beauty of it was tremendous.

All these precious moments together, made the bond between them ever so strong. Needing each other from one day to the next, they became good friends. Then months later, they fell in love with each other. Two wonderful people looking for a life full of miracles – and they found the biggest miracle of all – love. Many people search the world for this magnificent occurrence and never find it. Mami and Pappa were blessed to find one another.

Pappa was anxious to speak with the family to express his intentions concerning Mami. He first talked with Aunt Carmella, telling her that he loved Mami and wanted to marry her. Aunt Carmella advised Pappa to tell the head of the family of his intentions – Grandmom. So Pappa met with Grandmom to ask for Mami's hand in marriage. Grandmom's intention was to put up a little fight, but instead, she just fainted. After she came to, Mami told Grandmom how much she loved Pappa, so it was settled, and preparations for the wedding were set in place. They were married August 5, 1946. The precious island pearl and the soldier tied the knot.

It is so wonderful and gracious of our Lord when He sets his plans for two sweet souls to meet, fall in love, and be together for a lifetime. Everything just falls into place. The Lord knows who, when, and where. All hearts are softened and all is right, according to God's plan.

This lovely couple was married for 42 years. Pappa was called home to be with our Lord, while Mami lived on for 27 more years before she was called home to heaven and to her beloved husband. I have always been grateful for God's placing me in a home with such kind, good, and wonderful parents. They taught me so many good things about life. They will always be in my heart until we are together again, in heaven. Thank you, Jesus, for my loving parents, whose love for me had no end.

Mami at 10 years old

Father at 16 years old

Georgianna Zdunowski, 1 year old

A MOTHER'S UNDYING LOVE

It is a miraculous gift from God--He created
the concept of mothers. In my life it was a
tremendous and unique blessing. My mother
was, and still is, a woman of tremendous valor
in character and being. From the beginning of
my life she saved me from a doomed future. I
came into this world with the medical odds
against me. My birth was that of a premature
infant. During the 1940's, it was pretty risky to
have a premature child since chances of the
baby surviving were near zero. Each and every
day that passed by after my birth, the doctor

13

would tell my mother that I might not live very long. My bed was an incubator instead of a crib.

It was the dead of winter and my mother walked several miles in the bitter cold, every day, just to be by my side. Knowing that my life was uncertain, my mother would sit beside me, composed and confident. She would reach into the incubator where I laid, and touch my small body, a mere two pounds. She would caress my arms, legs, and tiny hands. Even though I was in a deep sleep, I could feel her touch filled with endless tears of hope. I knew someone needed me to live. If it were not for this beloved angel, I could have never survived. As the years passed, my mother never left my side.

We have had a unique, spiritual bond between us, from the beginning of my existence. This bond is always connecting us together and the strength of it is unbreakable. It seems that my life is filled with my mother's being. Even though I am old now, I still need her close, as if my survival depends on it. She fears nothing and puts all her love and faith in God. Her prayers are gentle as a butterfly's wings, humble as the color of a rose, and as strong as the presence of the high mountains. Her love conquers all snares and dangers for me. Her face is like the sunshine of a new day. I am ever so grateful to God for giving me such a wonderful mother, who is a strong warrior. I really needed her in this cruel and vast, empty world.

Just as her love is endless for me, I too love her with all my being. She is my trusted friend and companion forever. Our love for each other will go on without hindrance from this world. Thank you, beloved mother, for your undying love. Your daughter, from so long ago. I love you.

BEDTIME SONG-UN CABALLO TAN BONITO

(Our bedtime song written by Mami, 1951,
to Georgie, her doll, Kockeye,
and to Wally and his Teddy Bear, Poochie)

Blom, Blom.

Un Caballo tan
bonito
Para Montarlo mi
chiquito
Con facilidad
Que bonito caballito
Tan ligero, tan
chikito
Como correde
verdad
Upa, Upa, Upa
Caballito Alazan
Hey, Hey, Hey
No corrastanto
tediran
Vuelta aca, vuelta
alla,
Galopando mi
chiquito gozoran

A Beautiful horse
To ride my little
baby
With ease
Such a pretty horse
So fast, so small,

How he truly rides
Upa, Upa, Upa
Little horse, Alazan
Hey, Hey, Hey
Don't ride too fast,
Turn here, turn
there
Trotting my small
baby.
Enjoy it.
Blom, Blom.

Wally

16

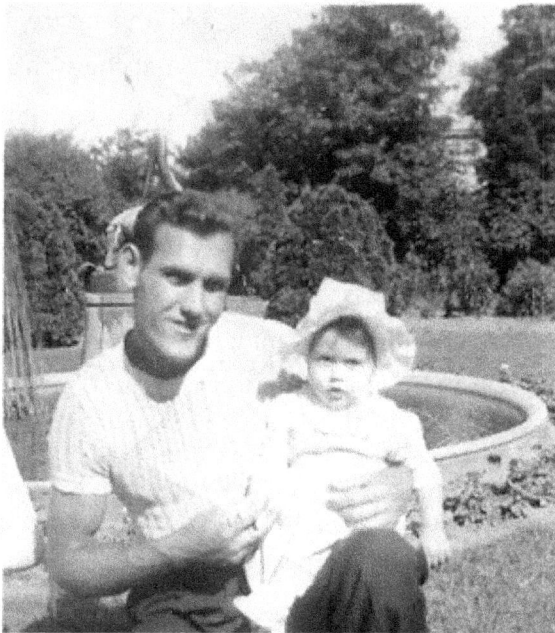
Georgie and Pop at the Park

A HOUSE WITHOUT A ROOF IS LIKE A CHILD WITHOUT A FATHER

Can you imagine living in a house that was built without a roof?

The house was built in stages. The foundation was poured and dried, the framing went up, the walls took form, the floors were laid, and the windows were securely installed. Suddenly, construction came to a halt. There was a mistake in the plan. **No roof**. Those who now live in the house unprotected wait for the workers to return to finish the job, but they never come. Time passes and the occupants never know from day to day what the weather will be. One day it is beautiful with clear skies, and they bathe in the warmth of the sun. But after a few hours, they long for shade from the intense heat. But with no way to escape the sun, an endless inferno of pain begins. Tomorrow, the sun may beat down again causing increasing deterioration and possible death.

On another day, out of the blue, a fearful tempest could come your way, destroying everything in its path. It shows no mercy as it tears away the bricks and lumber, destroying even the very foundation of your house. All that is left behind is a pile of ruins, broken dreams of your new home. If only you had finished the roof, providing additional protection against the horrifying effects of the villainous sun, wind, and rain. All the hard work that had been done to build the house could have been saved simply by adding a roof to the house. It would have given the ultimate protection against all the elements of the day.

Again, I wish you to imagine a home exposed to all the different and terrible storms that are possible and natural to life. When the winds howl, and rains have no end, when the snow reaches great heights, and gigantic-sized hail pounds down, when temperatures take a dive way below zero, a person would suffer immeasurably--possibly even resulting in death without the protection from these natural disasters. All could have been saved with the finishing touch of a roof, covering you and your house, creating safe shelter.

Now, look at this story from a different viewpoint. Leave the harsh reality of this world and go deep within yourself. Travel through the development of your physical life where you will be exposed to all forms of danger. You must be taught how to exist and fight in this world. Initially, being a helpless infant, some dangers and pitfalls of life cannot be fought by you alone. You will need your father's shield to protect you from all the evil of others in order to live. You were brought into this world with a sound and solid foundation-- your parents.

The walls are the paths in your life that you choose to take. The floors are your stepping stones, ensuring that the journey is on a safe footing. Our steps are always under the watchful eyes of our loving fathers, who are alongside of us as we undertake this perilous journey in life. His covering must be one of stupendous strength, vigor, and valor, enabling us to endure the hazards of this world. This is the main reason why God has provided us with earthly fathers. They are our teachers and champions, sheltering us, their children, from harsh verbal attacks from others. Never forget that a child's spirit can be broken and made unrepairable when subjected to destructive words and actions from others, including bad fathers. These repeated attacks can lead to spiritual and physical death of a child, without a good father to love, protect, teach, and guide the child throughout her life With him, the covering of your life is not complete, just as a home is complete with all the components in place for its protection, including the roof.

I thank You, God, each and every day, for the tremendous blessing of having a wonderful and beloved father. The home that our family lived in was complete and safe. The teachings taught to me will always remain in my heart, mind, and spirit. My father taught me love, kindness, generosity, and to be gentle to all. Although my father has passed away now, my memories of him still linger in my heart and spirit. I do not feel I would have had a strong foundation in life is I had had a different father, or no father at all.

My father was a champion in my life. God must have wanted me to survive to do His work as I had timeless protection from a caring father. May we see each other again. I love you always. Your daughter.

Wally and Pop in the Back Yard
Reading, PA, 1951

Georgie and her brother, Wally

FIRST FRIEND

My first friend in this life was my brother.
As I rummaged through some old photographs
of my past, I experienced a cloudburst of
tucked-away memories. As a little girl, I was
always hanging onto my best friend. I could
beat him up and my reward would be a big
hug. He would always be there for me,
protecting and shielding me from harm. This
was his main goal. My brother's days were
filled with endless mischief and plenty of
laughter. There were times that I would see a

twinkle in his eyes that truly surpassed the brightness of the sun. Feeling the warmth of his heart felt like crawling under tons of blankets on a cold, winter day... or better yet, sitting on the antique black cast-iron heating vent on the floor of our living room. My brother was my true hero of all heroes!

It sure was *The Life of Riley*, having a friend alongside you each moment of the day. Call it an endless slumber party. The attic of our home was two rooms filled with barrel-rolling contests, soldiers beating up the Indians with Lincoln logs, and of course the train ride to nowhere. Those were the days. Our minds were filled with unlimited, imaginative ideas and dreams only kings and queens dare to dream. Each new season that came upon us was filled with exciting adventures and the big question that lingered in our minds, "What kind of trouble lay waiting for us today?"

Our summers were always full and lots of fun. As each summer approached, my brother started looking for a worthy swimming opponent. But his plans changed, when instead, he had to play lifeguard and retrieve me from the bottom of the pool. Many times he would get a kick out of me seeing me start to sink; but he was always there to save me. I think the main reason he played lifeguard was because our Pop told him to be on the lookout for me. He could expect a whopper of a spanking if I would have drowned. But my brother surely enjoyed the whole ordeal; his laughter was heard all around and I thought it was worth a million dollars.

We would always travel together to see our grandparents in the summer. They lived in Puerto Rico. I remember one particular time, being served a meal on the plane. My brother was joking around as usual, when all of a sudden, instead of the food being on the tray, it was all over me. I thought to myself, what kind of impression am I going to make getting off the plane? Yes! I was a big mess, but what a good time we had laughing about it. Of course, the laughter did not start until I threatened to kill him. My brother sure did love to joke around, but it never turned out too damaging. Needless to say, he got off the plane looking like a million dollars, and I looked like a pitiful pig that just wallowed in his food pen. After that little incident, I never wore a dress on the plane again.

If we were not at our grandmother's in Puerto Rico, we would be back home sitting on the rooftop of our house, talking about anything and everything. Sometimes would dare each other to jump from our roof onto our neighbor's roof. But, of course, we never did it. We knew our parents would not be pleased with us. One particular day, my brother's mind switched directions. Benny, his friend, was coming over to see us and show us some gift he had just received. We talked over the plan and decided to fill up a large plastic container with water and wait until his friend showed up. Well, he showed up and we dumped the water right on top of him as he was looking up at us. It started to be funny at first, but then the laughter stopped. You see, we not only wet his face, but also his new suit. Not a good joke that day.

Once a year, the carnival would come to town, and my brother and I would be partners on all the rides. My brother was a champ on the rides, never getting sick. After a few rides, I would turn a beautiful shade of mint green, and boy did that make his day. It would get even worse in the fun house, which was more like the horror house from the haunted hill for me. Upon entering, he was neatly dressed, but as we would exit, his clothes were more wrinkled than an old dried-out prune.

On to Winter. We were always having fun in the snow, building tunnels all over the street and between the parked cars. During Christmastime, we would walk to Penn Street, downtown, with our parents to see the Christmas lights. All the stores would put light displays in their windows. We would go to Pomeroy's Department Store to shop. Our Mom would distract us while Pop would buy the presents. It was great when Mom and Pop would think we were asleep on Christmas Eve, and we would watch them carry the presents down from their secret place in the attic. Our parents would place the presents ever so gently under the biggest tree in the state, which filled our living room. Our Pop always tried to get us the best tree in town because he always wanted us to know that his love for us was as big as that tree. Our Pop's past Christmases as a child were not as loving and full of overwhelming joy as ours. It was truly a magical time for us and our parents made it all possible.

Springtime was a time for us to go the park and feed the ducks. Right before Easter, we would go to the basement of Grant's Store and look at all the baby ducks. It was a lot of fun for us as we could hold the ducks and wish we had one. One special spring our dream came true when our parents let us buy two ducklings. Boy! What a great feeling it was to be the proud owners of our own ducks. Our next thought was, "How much should we charge our friends to feed the ducks?" We had fun training them to walk on a leash and go everywhere with us, which fascinated our neighbors.

On Sundays, our normal routine was to go to church and then meet up with the extended family in the area at grandmother's house for dinner. Grandmother came from Austria and knew how to cook everything from scratch. Her meals were spectacular and delicious. She grew her own fruits and vegetables, and beautiful flower gardens in her immense back yard. She claimed the biggest cherry tree on the block. Since our house didn't have a backyard, we loved to explore Grandmother's vast farm-like backyard and enjoy all the wonders we found there. The only part of her backyard that wasn't wondrous was the outside bathroom, known as Grandmother's outhouse. As I sat in the outhouse, from time to time on our routine visits, my brother delighted to hang on its door, telling me stories about the snakes and bugs that lived in the hole of the outhouse. I sure was out of there fast!

As the years passed, my brother always stood by me, until it was time for him to start his own life. It was very difficult for me to let go of my best friend of seventeen years. At times, I thought my brother's main purpose in life was to aggravate me, like the undying gnat.

But to my advantage, my brother was teaching me how to stand up for myself. He spent seventeen years teaching me to be strong, so when the day came for him to leave, I could make it without him.

I am truly grateful to God for having had a friend throughout my early years of life, and it was a double blessing that it happened to be my brother. I only have my memories now of our life and times together, but the love was deeply imprinted within my soul, carrying me throughout my life. I wish my brother to know that he was the best and the first friend I had in this life.

Cousin Ruthie, Georgie, and brother Wally

725 MCILVAIN STREET

I grew up in a small city known as Reading, in the State of Pennsylvania. Reading was situated in a valley and nestled among rolling hills. Reading was not as colossal as Salt Lake City where I now live; it was on a much smaller scale. My parents, one brother, and I lived in a four-story, row house, consisting of 13 rooms.

As you entered the front door, you entered a long chamber which we divided into four rooms, starting with the living room. Walking a little further you entered what they today call the family room. Next was the dining room, and last was the kitchen. Off of the dining room was a flight of stairs leading down to the basement. In one room of the basement was our coal furnace. Along the right side of the furnace was a coal bin divided by several wood slats. One side was for the coal, the other side was for scrap wood and old newspapers. These items were needed, along with the coal, to start the fire in the furnace. The other room held my father's tools, neatly arranged on shelves. We also had an old-fashioned wringer washing machine across from the furnace that we used to do the laundry. That chore was a hard job for my mother and it took hours to accomplish. During the winter months, my mother would hang the laundry in the basement to dry. It was a great place to have adventures among the mysterious world created by the sheets and blankets, or exploring the bins and tools --all great inspirations for our young imaginations.

As you went up to the second floor, there was a bedroom straight ahead, which was my brother's room. To the right was the bathroom and on the landing, closest to the stairs was the door to my bedroom. Straight through my room was the entrance to my parent's bedroom. Off to the right of my bedroom was another flight of stairs leading up to the attic. The attic consisted of two bedrooms, but unlike all of the other rooms on the first and second floors, the attic had hardwood instead of linoleum floors. This made it possible to truly tap dance with much gusto; or when mom put down a good layer of wax, you could slide across both two rooms with your socks on. Add a little salt and you were ready for a good old polka dance. In the back bedroom was another doorway. This one led to the first level of the rooftop.

As you stepped out on the roof, it was like walking on black gold. When the sunlight reflected off the roof, it shined like gold. The roof was equally squared on all sides with the outer perimeter embraced by wood slats. The roof itself had tar paper sheets covering it. On the back portion of the roof, facing the backyards of the neighbors, there was an enormous chimney stack. It was a great place for my brother and me to sit beside each other and hang our feet off the edge of the roof and watch all the action happening in the alley behind our house. We could see the entire neighborhood for several blocks. There were two playgrounds within our view, two alleyways going in separate directions and of course, our friend's homes. It was a very diverse and versatile neighborhood, consisting of quite a few different cultures. We used to love to just sit out there on the roof and listen to the beautiful music that came from all directions of the alley.

We had a very close friend that was an inspiring, future musician who practiced his music on his back patio. He would always ask us what we thought of his new composition. He was very good. Once we watched an elderly gentleman turn a simple piece of wood into a striking guitar.

Another event that comes to mind was when a monkey escaped from a travelling circus and the monkey made its way to our neighborhood. He was jumping around on the electrical wires from one home to the other. It was a great view from the rooftop that day. The monkey sure had frizzy hair by the time the circus people caught him due to all the shocks he received from the live wiring.

There were times when you could smell the aroma of all the different meals that were prepared by the mothers and grandmothers. If you would lie on your back you could just about touch the clouds during the day, and at night the stars were so close you could pick one that you liked and put it in your pocket. On the Fourth of July, the view of the fireworks from the far-off park was absolutely superb.

My father loved birds of any kind, so one summer he built a large birdhouse for our newly purchased pigeons. The birdhouse was next to the large chimney stack and it was so big that my brother and I could climb into it along with the birds. We would go with our father to different parts of town, release the pigeons and they would always make it back home.

There was another level to the rooftop and during the summer months my father and brother would lie up there getting a fabulous tan. In order for you to get up to this upper level, you would have to climb up on the side wood slats with the help of a chair, but boy, what a view then. Once up there, you could go from your house to your next five neighbors' houses and hang out on their rooftops.

The rooftop of our home was a very special place to our family, friends, and their families. It holds many memories and great adventures for all who spent time on the rooftops. I know that people who live in the west have the mountains to cherish and reflect upon. Our roof allowed us to see many of God's wonderful sites, including his wonderful hand in all forms of creation. My brother and I really had good times together, and it was a very inspirational place for us.

SACRED LOVE

When you have the need for another and that need overflows, there is love between the two of you. You are no longer alone. Now you are two lives complete, each filling the others needs with true, unconditional love. One sacrifices for the other, trying to protect and nourish their beloved's soul, from all the misdemeanors of the world.

There is never a thought of turning back or turning aside, only complete devotion between you two. You live each day focused on the care and survival of the other. No risk is too great, no sacrifice is too small. The secret of life is to have your needs met by the overflow of your love for another soul, just like a mighty river overflowing its banks. Let your love be gentle and kind, without beginning or end. With no boundaries or conditions set, you give all you can to protect each other from the mistreatment of others.

Life will then have new meaning and your path will be covered with gold. Your love is strong enough to endure through the years. As your two lives intertwine with love and strength, sharing each passing moment of your lives together, you will actually know the truth of sacred love.

You can now easily imagine love as pure as a crystal and as strong as a rock, enduring till the end of time.

MY PRECIOUS BUTTERFLY

There is a spirit in my life that is as gentle and beautiful as the butterfly. Its soothing touch is as wondrous to me as the metamorphosis of the butterfly. The beauty of its luminous continuity of colors compares to the beauty of her soul. This elegant spirit is a precious lady, who happens to be my mother.

As a child growing up, there was never a need for fear, as my mother's loving being was always near. She protected me with all her might. Her strength seemed to be beyond my comprehension. Every living fiber of her being existed for her family. She never once considered herself over us or what harm she might be promenading into. If any blow of cruelty ever threatened to cross my path, she would shield my body and spirit by taking the full impact upon herself, whatever the cost. It is truly a gift from God to have such a precious and beloved mother. She has been my singular true and undying friend throughout my life.

No matter how many scars I accumulated over the years through the tormenting of others, my mother could heal the deepest and most devastating wounds left by my perpetrators. It seemed I would only get flesh wounds, while her spirit would encounter pieces of her life's fiber being torn away bit by bit, until finally the exposed marrow of her bones left her flesh disfigured.

This precious mother had a spirit as strong as the rocks embedded within the timeless mountains, while her love is as gentle as the wings of a butterfly. Her love for me will last for all eternity just like creation itself. If not for this gracious lady in my life, I would cease to exist. My life would have far less meaning and direction. I am ever so grateful to God for her love, strength, guidance, and powerful shield of security.

Now, although I am no longer a child, I still yearn for my mother's waiting arms, needing her immeasurable strength and courage. I compared her love and beauty to a precious butterfly. This was my father's loving affirmation and name for her, his "Precious Butterfly". As the butterfly aviates, you never even know it is there. The tranquil existence of this gentle pilot is like the existence of my mother, waiting for me in silence. Illuminating her beauty at every interval of my life, my mother is a great joy to me. She fills the emptiness of my soul just by being near me. Her love heals the ever-present wounds caused by this world. The endless emptiness of my days ceases as we share moments together, timeless friends from years gone by.

My spirit will always long for her presence to make my life complete and whole. I will always have a purpose to my existence with my mother beside me. Remember me, my precious little butterfly. You are my gift from God.

JOURNEY INTO LIFE

"He that dwelleth in the secret place of the most High shall abide under the shadow of the Almighty".

Psalm 91:1

R
✝

SEAL OF PERFECTION

You are who you are, with God's precious seal. Right from your start, God made plans for your life. No matter what path in life you take, you might choose the right trail early or it may take years for you to find out why God chose only you for that special task to be accomplished in your lifetime.

During your existence on this planet you can be the most important person, carrying huge standing in this world, accumulating many honors and medals, attaining walls of acknowledgement with the great work you have accomplished. You stopped at nothing to get to the top.

You can be a loving parent, working hard all your life to take care of your family. We are all the same, with dreams of accomplishment, doing something in our lives that will bring us happiness. We may sometimes be allowed to glimpse these wonderful dreams and go as far as to live them for a moment in time. Our essence is allowed to be totally consumed by our fantasies for the duration of whatever time is permitted. But God has set us in motion in

43

this world. We are who we are no matter how hard we try to forget, to ceaselessly fool ourselves. Our ultimate defeat is to force ourselves to be who we are not instead of whom we are meant to be. Go with the spontaneous gifts you were born with from the precious Divine above.

Excel to the max with all your might. You have the ability to reach for the stars. At times, you will be able to dream your dreams and share your happiness with others. Most of all, be who you are meant to be. God has created you spirit, body and soul. You have His seal of perfection, his stamp of approval. Your life is his instrument in this vast, fruitless world. Go forth with your signet and live your destiny with true dignity no matter what path God has chosen for you. You are the only one who can fulfill the mission that is placed upon you. Let your spirit touch others' souls, just as the wind touches your cheek.

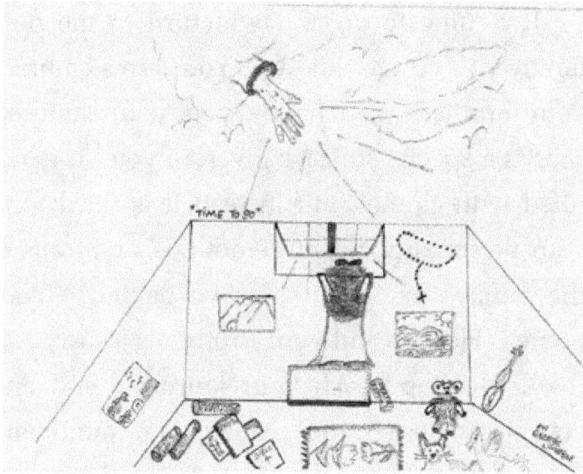

"Time to Go" by Georgianna Linnebur

THE TRIP

With suitcase in tow, you are just about ready to board. You will be going on a trip, your brother has told you. But first, you must say goodbye to your family. This trip is for you alone. But, there is a question that causes your mind not to rest. How long is this vacation? Is it a holiday trip, or could it turn out to be a nightmare for you? As your departure time comes closer, your mind cannot help but wonder, what will the strangers be like you will be visiting? What will their foreign home be like? Will it be nice or a trial to endure? Up to this point in your life, you have never been away from your treasured and precious family home.

It is time to go and you turn to the only family you've ever known. Your arms embrace your brother, who hands you your suitcase. This is a special suitcase given to you. It is not filled with clothes, but instead it is filled with your personality, talents, emotions, and traits of the family you have to leave behind. Your home is Heaven and your Brother is Jesus.

As you approach your journey's end and your new home, you realize your mind and heart will always ache for your home of old. You do your best to enjoy this transitory trip since it could last for a moment or two, or it might last for years.

But now, you are preparing for another trip. Before you can pack up your old suitcase with all the lessons you were able to learn from this place, so far away from your real home, you place pictures and letters in the suitcase so your Brother in Heaven can see what your trip was like.

Time is up and now you get to really go home. The fears and apprehensive feelings you felt coming on this trip are no longer on your shoulders. They are not an issue. All you feel is love and joy. You will be going to a place that you are very familiar with. It is your real home from the beginning of time. What stories you will be able to tell your family, spending hours sitting with your brother, talking of olden days and sharing all you have learned. As you see, time never moved since you started on your trip. All time ceased to exist and happened in a twinkling of your Father's eyes. To you, it seemed like days, then years. But your Father in Heaven sets the rules. His time is not earth's time. It is a special time for you to come full circle in your earthly life.

Welcome home with embracing love. You have been missed.

Drawing by Chris Linnebur, Georgie's Son

THE PATH

The road of a person is the route that they have to travel upon in their life. It will always be rough and bumpy, having potholes and ditches in it causing need for repair constantly. You will experience much sadness, disappointments, regrets and desires beyond reach.

But just like an old-fashioned dirt road, your life will be filled with many surprises, too. You never know what will be around the next bend. It has always been a known fact that if you have to go somewhere, there is really only one true way to go. There will be many paths on the side roads which can be taken, but only one is the true way. On your way to your final destination there will be many extra, pleasing sights to the eyes. But you must remember that they are only for you to look at and not to get caught or tangled up in. There will be times when you will have short delays in route. They are for teaching purposes in your life, so let the clock tick by and enjoy the ride.

You will also have other roads leading into yours, which God has purposely done in order for other lives to touch yours while you travel in this world. Your route has already been picked, just like other people have their own route from God to travel upon. You must trust God enough to help you on this perilous journey, as you cannot do it alone. God is your road map in life. Let his Grace glide you across the pitfalls and snares. You will have much opportunity to take many new paths, but let God be the navigator and steer you along the way. Then you will never feel the true impact of the damaged road under your feet.

WHAT YOU HAVE WITHIN,
YOU CAN HAVE WITHOUT

Imagine all that lies within the mysteries of the Universe. Without the touch of the Spirit, you cannot understand all the reasoning behind the magic of its wonders. At times, it is almost spellbinding to be in deep thought about the beginning and ending of all the creation in the heavens and on the earth. What makes a new star glow deep in the heavens or cause the first breath of a human being or an animal? It is the power that comes from deep within that makes the impossible become possible. If you are without that power and hope, there are no promises or possibilities. What is it that a mother holds deeply within her heart for her family? If you are without a mother, you may think the deep feelings of love are not there and your life is forever empty as the silence of a tomb.

Our Creator and Father in Heaven gave us the gift to be able to feel love and believe in miracles, deep within our spirits. We will have a greater understanding of all living things with this gift. If you are without the Spirit, you will never know what it is to love and to understand the true meaning of life and the universe. It is up to you to choose to have the ability be within, or you can choose to be without it. God's dreams and knowledge can be yours or you can choose to be an empty vessel, just living one day to the next, waiting for the silence to end within your spirit, without knowing love, without knowing God. The promises are there from your Creator. All you have to do is trust and believe in God, and the world will open up its arms for you to celebrate.

Many individuals live in a black and white world, not knowing the truth of all things. When you live in this environment, you have no thoughts of your own. All is routine and you walk upon the earth as the walking dead. These people are afraid of what they do not know which makes new beginnings unapproachable for them. The spiraling illiteracy of their lives never ceases. There are no books of knowledge in their world, nor do they crave the desire to learn from them.

In the same existence of time, there are people living with knowledge of the world. They help others to understand the universe and its true purpose. The course of learning to love and care for each other is an important development in the growth of an individual. You must be willing to accept changes with an open heart. There will no longer be blank pages in your life. You will have substance to digest with your mind and heart.

A black and white soul is similar to a mechanical robot, dull and lifeless is its being. It has no thoughts or ideas of its own. It is just an empty shell, giving nothing and expecting nothing. Its mind is programmed to do as it is told and never cross the line. The prismatic soul has thoughts, feelings and meaningful purpose. Its need for knowledge has no limits and there is no end to the undying thirst to learn and experience the wonders of the universe. This kaleidoscopic soul is honored and eager to share its world with the black and white soul. Once you learn the reasoning behind the universe, you can possess honest values, along with the awareness of life. Your heart will bloom just like the folds of a flower opening. This unfolding process is a precursor to awareness and permanent knowledge which lasts a lifetime. With each exposed, opening petal, new insights arise within your heart, mind, and soul.

Unwillingness to learn leaves doubt, anger, and total deformity to your soul. There is no room left for understanding, and people become an annoyance to you. In time, your darkness becomes an endless grave. You become unreasonable and any serious consideration of unfolding of your heart becomes taboo. This decision makes it inevitable for a new life to ever exist. You are forever in a gray solitude, with all roads leading nowhere. There is no growth in your being, just a negative ignorance of a true life. The unfolding petals of your heart are not allowed to open, and if it were to open, it would do so abruptly, causing the channel of awareness to wilt and die in your life. It is up to you to be part of God's plan of prismatic life or choose to live in the pit of ignorance where the windows of your soul are only blank reflections.

THE SEED

There was a man who noticed a dead leaf on a table top. He proceeded to pick up the leaf, and as he held it in his hand, he decided to break the leaf apart. To his amazement, when he did, hundreds of tiny seeds fell into his hand. He marveled over the thought of this tiny seed, producing a tree of enormous magnitude. And it all started from a tiny seed planted in the ground. This man was totally awed at his discovery.

But, standing alongside him, another person had noticed something different. Instead of the seed growing into a tree, he saw the seed as a person and that as the seed grew into a tree, it cast a great shadow on the ground. He could see that this shadow represented all the lives touched and changed by this one person

Last of all, both men understood that nothing would have been possible without the help of the Holy Spirit living within the seed. He is the one who causes growth and makes it possible for us to help others.

By Chris Linnebur

FROM SOMETHING DEAD, THERE IS LIFE

As you travel through a desert, you may wonder why this wilderness of barren land has been forsaken and abandoned. The thought crosses your mind that maybe this land is unneeded, with little or no purpose. Maybe it has breathed its last breath and has departed from life. You become like a tenement of clay, feeling the shades of death all around you, as you travel deeper into this desolate, solitary landscape.

Then, the thought comes to your mind that maybe this land is just asleep and has not yet been launched into eternity. It is just like a mother's love brings her unborn child to life, trying to keep this gentle child's body and soul together. Your mother becomes your life's blood and you are her miracle from God. Life then is a creation of God. He not only quickens the life and flame in people, He is the Creator of all forms of life. The vital force is resurgent and given vivification from God.

The desert land was once merely asleep, but is no longer a barren wasteland. It has become a beautiful, sweet-smelling garden of wildflowers coming from the cactus and the ground itself. All is in bloom, and the birds sing a new tune just as the desert is new with life. Never dismiss something that looks dead, as gone forever. Let God show you how His love can work miracles in this world and in your life.

Georgie on her way to Betty's House, 1989

THE HOUSE OF PRAYER

It was a very cold winter day when I chose to take my morning stroll. The snow was up to my thighs and no other footprints were in sight. I was the first to make a path in this beautiful winter wonderland. The trees were glowing like silver, due to the snow freezing on the branches – a true winter miracle – right out of a Norman Rockwell painting. The cold, crisp morning air felt like you were being embraced by a waterfall.

As I walked in the high snow, dodging numerous trees in my path, my eyes caught a quick glimpse of the most beautiful place I had ever seen. I knew I had to get closer. I felt as if I were drawn to this spot like a magnet to metal. Approaching this wondrous log home, I noticed a beam of light, an illuminating aura, all around the house. It was as beautiful as the evening aurora borealis in the Alaskan sky.

As I drew closer, one room in particular caught my attention. The light it radiated seemed to come directly from Heaven. The brightness was ever so blinding. The strength of the light was like the sun when you look at it directly. The lighted room emitted a warm embrace over your shoulders so you were no longer alone or cold.

My curiosity was as strong as a mountain lion. I proceeded to look into the glass room, and there kneeling on the cement floor was a woman of unbelievable spiritual strength. The light around her was like a ring of angels, singing and dancing. The prayers she offered up to heaven for others were being heard. This marvelous lady never gave a thought to herself, just offering daily prayers for others, wanting their deep, concealed wounds of life to be healed. The path to this house was to hold an answer to the many beclouded wounds my own spirit embraced. My life would be penetrated by this light of prayers for many years to come. But all I knew that day was that I had to learn more of this precious lady who prayed in the light.

It truly was meant for me to venture through the snow and come upon this wonderful house in the woods, at the end of the road, in the midst of the wilderness. This beautiful lady and I have shared many good memories and discussions about the Lord. Although many years have passed since that first special day, I can still hear the Lord telling me about this House of Prayer. Betty is the lady's name, and she still kneels in prayer for others. Her prayers are lifted up to the Lord without ceasing. Betty has a great love in her heart for all in need. The Lord has given her a mission of prayer. She is known as a prayer warrior for Jesus. God bless my friend, Betty.

My journey to Alaska was drawing to a close. I was preparing to leave this beautiful land the Lord had created with utmost perfection. The truck I was driving was a mockery to my husband's family, who scornfully declared breakdown and curse on it. But upon hearing their comments, my friend Betty, anointed our old Suburban before we departed. Surprising to us, but not to Betty, we not only covered the 500 miles to our destination, but the Holy Spirit extended the life of the old car to go 200,000 miles beyond, before the vehicle was put to rest. Betty understood the power of prayer on our car when she anointed it as a true gesture of love.

The road to Betty's log house had a dual purpose that day. It was a journey for me to know the Lord better, building my faith with every word. And the road led to a precious friend's house, giving me rest and peace from the wounds that afflicted my soul by this world. May the Lord be forever with this Angel of Prayer. May her days be filled with His loving grace.

Betty's House in Wasilla, Alaska

By Chris Linnebur

THE BEACON

A soul is consumed by life's disappointments at times. Your true self finds it difficult to surface, due to the fearful impact which is brought upon you. Your divine gifts and talents are tossed around like the waves in a turbulent ocean storm until your battered spirit sinks to the dark, endless depth of the ocean floor. You are permanently lodged tightly into the muck and mire of the sandy floor of the vast ocean. Your new home is numbness and despair, never being able to surface again. The sand is your tomb, but only if you allow it to be.

Some souls are fortunate enough to surpass and make their gifts shine while others have a two-fold portion of life's difficulties. Their souls are bombarded just as rapidly as a series of bombs destroying a home, leaving nothing behind but bits and pieces of a fully-constructed spirit. The battle will be endless, but you must fight with all your might to have your talents surpass the stones tossed at you each day. Do not be consumed by tragedy. Let your true self remain intact so that others see the gifts God bestowed upon you, being able to enrich their paths with some of the radiant light given to you so long ago. You are truly helping others from the path of self-destruction. God will always give you the courage that is necessary to conquer and defeat the agony of this life.

It sounds truly wonderful to succeed in all that you do in life, but that cannot give your character a sound foundation. We need alarming situations for the mortar in our foundations to be able to take the blows of life. The outcome can make you a stronger, more giving person, with a deeper spirit soul in this life. Let your being shine like a beacon light in a weary storm for all to see. With all of God's grace poured upon you, you will survive and others will acquire strength from your example of life. Just believe that God has been, and always will be, there for all of you. Be one of His beacons in this vast toil-worn world.

By Chris Linnebur

PRISONER OF DARKNESS

Imagine yourself walking down an alley at night. The frigid walls surrounding you at eventide are ever so present and foreboding. No matter where you turn, the same darkness follows you and there is no escape. Darkness is forever plotting and planning deceitful deeds against you. Every approaching corner holds some new way to destroy your being. The crevices of darkness can strip away your physical being, leaving only a zombie-like carcass.

As your physical being is absorbed into the darkness, the very core or spirit of your being is attacked violently with utmost silence. No light is allowed to enter this maddening world, as it truly thrives upon the evil within. Only the light can destroy this immense cruelty upon your fragile being. Evil is strong and cannot be tricked. It listens to your every word and watches all your moves. You feel you must do its bidding or death is imminent.

All humans have the ability to overcome darkness, but many choose not to bother. It is much easier for them to be controlled by forces that are ever so enticing and materially rewarding. These dark forces make it possible for a human to please others in a very sinister way. We are merely driven to think that our minds are so weak and there is no other way.

But lo and behold, we do have a choice to make our life better. Don't be afraid to overcome the darkness. You must battle to find beauty and perfection, yes! The battle is unbearable at times, but you can succeed. You must know that darkness is not the way. Life is meant to be lived and not controlled by fear or ignorance. Light does not plot and plan for your destruction. On the contrary, it works towards your good. What you can do for others without the lies and corruption is far worth the reward. It completes your soul and makes you whole with a total understanding of life.

Do not ever fear the darkness as if it were your greatest enemy. You have the power within yourself, given to you from God, to destroy darkness from your life. And you have the power to help others to step out of their fearful environment. This is the gift that the Creator has given to you! The bonds of darkness can be forever lifted from your soul and your prison changed into the light of heavenly gardens. Others await their arrival into this new world, carried there due to your help and their awakening to the light.

THE FAMISHED BODY
OF AN OBEDIENT SPIRIT

A storm is converging around you. Is darkness inhabiting your soul? No, it is just the arrogance of death attacking your spirit. When a being allows evil into their life to take over without a fight, the storm of death will slink in rapidly. You are like a gentle animal being led to slaughter. You are just sitting back, being silent, and waiting for your gruesome fate by a very callous servant of evil. The situation can develop into the direction of being too afraid to ask others for strength, to battle an immense horror of deceitfulness alone. Do not be frightened; no spirit is too evil for you to just perch and you do their bidding. You must get all the help you can to destroy the hold this evil has on you.

Fear is no longer a factor in your daily life, just the permanence of honesty, goodness, and survival. Do not let the restoration of madness be resurrected from the ashes of hell in your life.

All you have to do is just turn the key in your life and all the evil that binds you will pass. You are not meant to be in servitude to the dark images of this world. There are multitudes of beings that cannot turn the key.

They have forgotten that there is still the beauty of kindness, the color of love, and the gentleness of trust in this world. Their minds have been altered, and they just live in fear everyday of their lives, knowing no difference.

God is here. He does exist. He is right next to you. All you have to do is turn the key to make the change. No one has the right to keep anyone in the chains of fear, not knowing why they are, who they used to be, or what they are, preventing them from coming into God's glory. All of these limitations transpire because you are trying to be obedient to another, not knowing that your spirit becomes famished the longer you let this change continue in your life.

Just walk away and set your eyes and path in God's direction. God will remove the chains that bind your soul and you will see again.

PROFOUND SADNESS

Chores are done; you are just doing some extra surprises to make another person's life happier -- trying to take the dark moments of life from thought and heart. Maybe there can be a few moments of light and happiness.

Then, just as sudden as the monsoon storm coming in, without any warning, an intense heavy-heartedness comes upon you in your moment of happiness. A look starts off as a glimpse towards you, then you get the glaring stare which is like a knife cutting into your very spirit. Once the conversation is started, blaspheming words are placed upon your being. The once kind face which looked upon you moments ago now has a countenance of uncontrollable rage.

The words are unhallowed and razor-sharp. Your spirit is sent to the bowels of the earth, submersed into an abyss by heartfelt woe. Your mind is in a tailspin and you are instantly plunged into an atmosphere of a desecrated realm. Your feelings and spirit have been viciously attacked by the abnormalities of another person's mind.

To keep yourself from further inhumane damage, you remember the memories of olden times --a hug, a smile from family and friends, a kind word or sweet gesture from a precious well-wisher. These memories are stored deep within your mind. Those happy memories help you get through the insanity of this cruel moment.

As time passes, all returns back to normal and the evil glance is gone for a moment, but only until the next intense downcast is placed upon you again. Your life is bombarded by sadness continuously, all of which is done by someone who has no profound purpose towards you.

Lift up your eyes from this tormented prison and see the light that is forever around you. Jesus is that Light, protecting and strengthening you. He will get you through your ordeal, that unnecessary, polluted aura that surrounds your sacred soul.

There is hope in the Lord. He will remove the sadness and abuse, providing you with profound love without end. He will cradle you with all His glory. Prayers will be answered and a new life will begin to emerge from the ashes of sadness.

TO BANISH JOY

When you have joy expelled from your life, you are left with a vacuum of emptiness. It is a prelude to sheer madness. Your spirit which felt gaiety and joy from the simplicity of a rose bush coming to life, the beautiful whisper of the wind touching your face, the long-lost arms of a loved one holding you close...they all disappear, leaving you feebleminded, enclosed in an unconcerned brick room.

The smells and colors of your old life are nonexistent. Now, only cold air, stale and pungent with the odor of death, comes from the mortared walls of your new life. This room in which you now live, was not your desired home. It belongs to another who thought his life had no further purpose. He thought it was in his best interest, from a delusional high standing above you, to dismiss this unique and precious individual, to a life of inhumane solitude. He and other strangers wished to banish joy and hope from this precious being, expecting the result to lead to your total madness.

UNCEASING SILENCE

Has there been a span in your life when you felt you could have lived in a space that was as silent as the empty air surrounding your being? After a long duration in this lifestyle, your soul beckons for the utterance from another earthling, but to no avail. The arrogance and unmerciful silence knows no end. The earthling must teach its spirit to be tolerant of this situation and prepare itself for the journey of long suffering. WHO IS THE EARTHLING HERE?

At times, the moments turn into desolate hours, leaving you in seclusion, causing your mind to race at a high velocity. If you cannot adjust to the ever-present predicament, the decomposition of your body and soul begin to take place. Your body is famished and lays heavy-hearted. Your spirit bellows for the termination of your plight. Death is like a heavenly garden that awaits your footsteps. There is an unceasing longing for pity from the Highest of the High, and your spirit depends on restoration to go on. A shift. Now, the endless silence of your life can no longer destroy you as your liberation lies in the precious hands of the Creator.

By Chris Linnebur

LIVING IN DARKENESS

While on a camping trip to Maine, I noticed that the birds in the forest were filled with much delight once the morning sun reached their frail little bodies. As they sat upon the branches of the stupendous trees, they bathed themselves in the warmth of the sun and seemed so content they became totally ecstatic. The songs they sang were like the music that only angels could sing in the high heavens above. During the evening hours, right before nightfall, the birds sang their joyful songs again to each other as a finale of their day. It was a symphony to surpass all symphonies, as the elegant music moved from one tree to the next. Once darkness set in for the night, all went quiet. Not one beautiful, rejoicing wave of music was heard throughout the forest by these wondrous birds. It was as if these marvelous creatures went into hiding because of nightfall.

People are about the same when it comes to darkness. They become frightened and all they can think to do is to hide. If we could only realize that the light that Jesus radiates is with us all the time, there would be no need to fear the darkness ever again. The sounds of joyous music could be endless. You would be living in the light, and the darkness would be nothing to ever fear again. The circle of light would remain with you throughout your life and the wondrous sounds of the birds would never end as darkness falls.

Are you a drifter, wandering aimlessly all of your life? Are you finally getting to the point of not knowing the difference between what is genuine and what is make believe in your life? Your survival is held together only by your memories of true reality. In your life you have drifted too long and do not know how to get back.

At times, the faded memories that have given you love, kindness, and understanding, are set adrift into this endless spiral of nothingness. There are many times when you feel that your life has no meaning or future. You are totally absorbed with your life as a tumble-weed. Drifting from one place to another, you never feel any peace of mind in your decisions. You have made yourself lost, without anchor.

Then, without warning, you see yourself taking a glimpse at the twisting tornado of good memories, hoping that they can help you back to the truth. Maybe you will be jolted like a bolt of lightning onto a new path. Or, maybe you will have no reaction and remain in the wilderness of life--forever searching mysteriously in the storm, directed sporadically by your far-away dreams for the truth in life.

Provisions will be available to you to find your way back no matter how far you have drifted. Your memories will no longer be a lifesaver only in dreams, but memories will rise from the ashes just like the legendary phoenix. So, there is hope for you and a purpose for your life.

HIDDEN CHAINS OF THE SOUL

Why does man have such a colossal insensibility towards other human beings and towards the wondrous land where he lives? Even as a child, I could never figure out why different races chose to wedge animosity between themselves and others not like them. If only they would get along, respecting each other for who they are. We are all the same, with feelings deep within us, longing for peace, happiness and tranquility for our lives and the lives of our families. There is so much we can learn from each other if we give it a chance. Time has proven that the hate and inhumane acts of violence still live in our midst and touch all of our lives. It does not matter what monetary level you dwell at, satanic emotions can come into play. The demoralizing effect can eventually take a toll even from a person with a kind face who doesn't give our differences a second thought, leaving behind more hatred for each other.

A person seems to be just frothing, waiting for his next victim to appear. It is so outlandish how one human being can have no love or compassion for a fellow brother, or for the precious land that we live upon. The blood that runs from a body after a senseless beating is like a polluted river. And destroying a person's property is just as harmful as if they struck the person themselves with a whip. The outcome of these acts results in hidden feelings that have no love intertwined within the person's soul. In turn, no love or respect for another is displayed, which only leads to unbridled actions against a good soul.

My thoughts now go back to the Civil War era. My heart aches for the cruelty that was so freely meted out. It was nothing to strip a person of his clothing, baring his nakedness to all, and never giving his dignity a second thought. Continuously tearing away at this good soul for some insane gratification, persons with no moral values stripped away his humanity, until the victim lives no longer. They say those days are over and long forgotten, but are they really? In some dark corner of the world's closet you will hear, from time to time, the same degeneracy of another individual or domain happening.

Truly valuable time is being stolen from lives due to others' ignorance concerning the true meaning of sharing each other's life for the good of humanity and not for annihilation of people and lands. If only we could learn from each other and become who we were meant to be, putting aside all the past mistakes and truly caring for each other. We could look forward to a new way of life together.

Each person you look upon is a masterpiece created by God. All the beauty in this land leaves you with one breathtaking feeling after another. Why then would you ever want to destroy the elegance that God created for us to love and enjoy? Everything was put here for a good purpose and intent, not for destruction resulting in obliteration. We truly must learn at some point that we need each other. The time is now when it comes to treating each other with dignity. Let the past mistakes burn a memory in your soul...that we must be better and strive for a good life for all mankind, as God has always purposed it to be.

By Chris Linnebur

FOOTPRINTS IN THE WATER

It had been a summer of lengthy dog days that particular year. At times, you could feel the torrid heat that would never end. Then, as an answer to many prayers, a cloudburst of rainfall came your way. Soon, the steady rainfall turned into a monsoon and you became drenched and sopping wet to the skin. The only thought that comes to your mind is to jump deliriously and with the utmost gaiety from one puddle to the next, splashing water far and wide. Now at this point, you are totally into the submersion of cool refreshing rainwater.

Of course, all good things come to an end. The sun came back out and peeked its rekindled flame around the dark clouds. All of a sudden, your moment of merriment is concluded and you are swept back into the never-ending heat wave of the summer. All that remains of your brief memory of the rain are small pools of water separated by the hot, dry cement. As you paused for an instant, you noticed that your feet left impressions everywhere on the dry cement. All this wet graffiti was produced from the puddle of rain you were celebrating in. You left behind footprint upon footprint, in every direction. The cement came to look like someone was totally confused, not knowing which way to go. Based on the footsteps, they just kept changing their trodden way, hoping that the next route would take them to their desired destination. The route was always the same, with crisscrosses over each other, going in circles to nowhere and never exiting onto a straight path.

A deeper thought now forms, that the footsteps reveal how a person's life truly is. They never know which direction in life to choose, so it turns out like the mixed-up footprints in the water, going in all directions, never getting anywhere in life and accomplishing little. If only all of us could be aware of the true fact that when you put Jesus in charge of your life, there would not be so many paths going in different directions and ending up in an endless circle. Jesus will set you on the true path that He chooses for you--a straight and direct line in your life, from the beginning to the end. No more confusing paths--just a life open to God's pathway and not our own.

PLAY THE MUSIC

The need to survive is fulfilled by living off happy memories. The memories need not be yours alone. After others are gone, the necessity of their good and happy moments in life are replicated into our lives. On the other hand, it might not have to be as drastic as someone's death for this replication to transpire in our lives. Any good that has been done before or after our birth, never dies. It is just transmitted to another person through past and present works and accomplishments. There is a strong need to live and if it takes a glimpse of someone else's joy, it is done.

The legacy of another person can become the lifeline for another's soul. The harshness of one's life is set aside for a few moments and you are allowed to feel the love and freedom of your youth. It often lasts just long enough to sustain your soul and rejuvenate your life. This particular act of love and kindness makes you strong enough to go back to the realities of your life. Like an uplifting song, you now have more strength, a better appreciation for life, and you are glad to be where you are. It is good to have these moments of a melodic, adoptive legacy to carry us through life's most difficult times. Let the music play. It is one of our gains in this world when sweet sounds soothe our souls to goodness. Then we can radiate the joy we feel.

By Chris Linnebur

WHAT DOES IT MEAN TO EXIST?

"You do not exist!" Oh, how those four simple words can truly incise your soul to the quick.

To be non- existent, a non-person, must cease to exist, pass away, die out, be no more, be uncreated, gone, and finally be lost forever. I can assume that the above covers "not exist" pretty conclusively on all sides of life. On the other hand, to exist is to be present, to breathe, live, stand, to prevail, and to ultimately endure life's tribulations, which happens to us from time to time.

Now the reason for this story is because it all started out to be a simple day for me, sitting in front of an insurance agent. She leaned forward to tell me that even though I was sitting in front of her, I did not exist.

Please explain the situation more.

Okay. I know in my soul that I am still alive. I have a mother that loves me and she can provide undisputed evidence that I am a person of strong essence living in this foreign land. My trail of existence is leaving its mark on all that it touches. According to this material world, if you have no credit, bills, or checking account, you merely and plainly, do not exist. You are ejected within a blink of the eye from the life of mankind. At this point, the sphere that encompasses your life is now considered a vacuum. It sure does make you wonder at times, how coldblooded the human race can be. Amid this insanity and sadness, it is such a blessing to know that God is in charge of our final assessment. God would never abandon us or annihilate us off the surface of the earth, even if a person suffers loss in their life. We live in a very unrealistic world and their way of life is not true. We must always remember that no matter what happens, always be kind to others. They need recognition and validation in their lives just as we do. We go on struggling; trying to do our best in a cold world, until God calls us home. Otherwise, don't let anyone mislead you. You have value and you do exist.

By Chris Linnebur

A DEAR PRICE

What is the true price we pay in order to have and possess material things? Aside from the money or price tag, what is the real cost involved? And what are you expecting the material possession will bring you? So many times, the need we are trying to fill is not satisfied by a new car, a new suit, or a bigger house. In order to fill this need, the real desire and the true price are very clear. We clearly need another human being. All superficial pursuits of life disappear with each new longing. You need to be needed. The need for you to care for another human's welfare dissolves and displaces the desire for hollow and empty collections of material junk.

Just to see a family member or dear close friend smiling at you is worth more than a statue or an expensive trinket or portrait sitting on your shelf. To hear your mother softly humming is more warming and comforting than a shawl around your shoulders on a cool fall evening. Let your heart unfold to a new knowledge of true wealth just like the folds of a rose gently open on a warm, spring day. It is not the accumulation of wealth that causes you to reach this new awareness, but the value you place on the family and friendships in your life.

With each unfolding layer of your heart, the portrait on the shelf becomes another life for you to love and care for--those right there under your roof. The shawl becomes your mother's arms with undying love. The cold winter days become warm summer days, filled with visits from all close and far away.

Each nook and crevice of your home is no longer filled with emptiness, but with the precious, sweet voices of your loved ones. They are holding you and making your life full of riches that can never be bought. Yes! The price for true riches is clear and their loss can never be replaced. Let your heart be open to the unfolding of true love. It will carry you through your entire lifetime.

By Chris Linnebur

SHADOWS OF THE PAST

It was an hour before sunrise and the morning sky was crystal clear with a very brisk ambiance. The pale, blue-gray firmament embraced the lightly-brushed, snow-covered mountains of the east benches. As you gazed at this peaceful and serene sight, you noticed the beautiful array of bright lights coming from the dwellings lodged deep within the fractures and crevasses of the mountains. Lo and behold, these valleys are no longer the valleys of the mountains, but they are the deep valleys of your mind. The lights that you observed are now the memories of your life. Some lights may shine brighter than others, while other lights may cover a larger area. The larger and brighter the light, the more impact the memory has had in your life. These memories could be from a vast variety of experiences. Some could embrace your family of yesterday, and some from today. Maybe there will be places tucked away for safe-keeping, or an unforgettable moment that lightens your heart. There could be a legion of hopes and dreams, well hidden within the folds of your mind.

As you glance again at the dark silhouette of the mountains, you see a portion of darkness. There are no brilliant lights superimposing the massive elevation, just the emptiness of the frigid morning, reflecting off the somber, steep cliffs of the mountain. These silhouettes of the mind are from people who choose to have no yesterday or tomorrow. There are no memories for them of their past. They are here today, and have no hopes and dreams for tomorrow. Dreams have no place or time in their hearts and minds. Their plan is to just live life as a joyless adventure, anxiously waiting for the final stillness of the dark to permanently end their existence. Maybe this darkness could be from someone who has not been given a choice. They no longer live in this world or in God's world either. They lay still, waiting for the grim reaper to take away their final breath. There are no memories for them, just empty valleys within their minds.

These mountains in the dawn of the day are not just the incarnation of soil and rocks. They are the shadows of your mind, past and ever present. Do I dare stretch it far into the future! Your choices in life make the brilliance of the lights. Which memory is brighter than others, only your heart knows.

Now the morning sun is rising; dawn is taking its leave. The dark silhouette of the mountains has disappeared. You can no longer see the memories of your life. It is morning and the time has come to make new memories from the shadows of the past.

DESERT ROSE

While in Arizona, you will be fortunate to
see the beauty of its desert terrain. Among this
beauty lies a mysterious rock formation. Look
closely and you will see this beauty of a gem
snuggling next to the sagebrush, tumbleweeds,
and the over-towering Saguaro cactus. The
anatomy of this rock configuration is that of an
elegant rose. The petals are well-defined and

its color depends on the minerals the earth's soil contains in that certain area. The particular rose I saw there was the most beautiful red-pink color you could imagine. The inner and outer core of this delicate flower is made of rock. Its growth does not come from a green stem but, would you believe it, another rock. When the precious rose is fully formed it drops off of the extremely deformed base rock, leaving an imprint on it of a twinkling star. I am awed by this wondrous creation from God above. The beauty of this rose is enchanting and breathtaking. The sight of this wonder never leaves your mind.

My first summer in Arizona, I had the honor to meet a lady who was as beautiful as this desert rose. She had a fragile exterior, just like the petals on the rose. But her inner core was as long-standing and strong as the rock itself. Your chance of being able to meet such an individual, with such fine qualities, is rare. Just as rare as it is to find a desert rose. I was blessed to have a long, loving friendship with her by the grace of God. Her personality was the combination of my own father--polite, gentle and as soft-spoken as my Aunt Jennie. We spent many hours together, sharing the good moments, along with the bad. We talked of anything and everything; there was no end to our friendship. If I was scared, her arms were always open and the hug was there. She gave me the courage to go on when life was at its bleakest for me. There were times when I could gently fall asleep in her arms as she told me stories of her life. I always knew that I would be safe when she was around. Ironically, it was my responsibility to take care of this fine lady, as a home-care provider. But as it turned out, we took care of each other.

Years have passed and now all three of my teachers--my father, my Aunt Jennie, and my friend in Arizona, have passed on to a better life. They live within the loving embrace of God's arms. The love of my father is spiritual and the memories of our life together are tucked away, deep within the folds of my heart, never to be forgotten. The teachings of my Aunt Jennie are no longer a conversation. They are imprinted within my soul and will last my entire lifetime. The love, friendship, and companionship of my precious friend lie deep within the universe. I will never forget what we meant to each other, and I will always long for those open arms. I am thankful to God for allowing this wonderful lady in my life. I feel that everyone needs to have a desert rose in their life. Mine was a real Irish rose from Cork, Ireland.

The autumn time of year is always filled with undeniable beauty. The trees are an endless diverse array of colors. Who would ever think that these beautiful and vibrating changes would be a prelude to death? The chronometer of the seasons in nature is quite the same as the timepiece of a human being's life.

It is a wonder to once see brightly colored leaves, shining on the tree branches and then within a few short weeks, all the leaves lay lifeless and colorless on the shivering harvest ground. Autumn leaves ascribed on the crisp earth are as numerous as the human bodies that are laid to rest beneath the frigid surface, in a year's time, serving as their final home.

Winter brings a dormant time for nature. It is almost the same as a new life, waiting in the heavens to be born.

The springtime brings warmth so the gentle season of birth can come into being. The warm arms of God's love help the buds to grow. The springtime of a person's life is when they are old enough to love and share their life with someone and have children.

In the summer months, nature thrives and multiplies. It is living to its full potential. A human's summer is living their life, doing all that is necessary to exist, raising their families, forging generations to come. This is a time for humans to learn the rules of heaven and earth and to teach their children right from wrong. These years pass by rapidly. Parents keep their fingers crossed, hoping all goes well and that they are getting the rules of the universe right.

When fall sets in, the leaves on the trees are giving their last statement before death. They are old, but at their best. The bright and beautiful colors are the last of the love they can give to this world. As a person goes through the autumn of his life, he has completed all the tasks that were asked of him. It is time to sit back and shine as bright as an evening star, guiding others for the very last time. As the fall season ends, the leaves complete their cycle, gently gliding back to mother earth, while a person's spirit sits quietly in God's forever-loving arms. The return is slow and gentle, facing the Creator of all life, waiting for another level of seasons.

THE DEPTH
OF YOUR SPIRIT

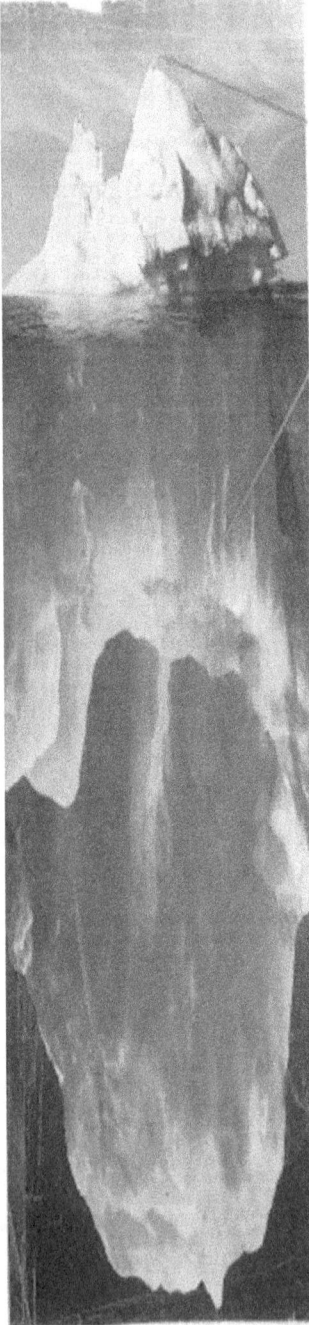

At times, only another person can see your outward spirit. But only God knows the depth of your true spirit within, which is rooted at the very core and composition of your being. You have been imprinted with a special seal, which, in turn, is like a seed growing in your soul. Forever struggling to grow to its greatest potential, this seed pushes itself to go further towards endless possibilities. We truly do not have a great knowing or understanding of this spiritual phenomenon happening in our being. But all is determined by what you allow yourself to be, as it was meant from the beginning of time. God will provide all the spiritual nourishment necessary for you if you let Him in.

God will strengthen your spirit and give it the main ingredients necessary for it to soar and swell. The bond between you and the Lord will be woven together, never to be severed by anyone or anything. It is not a mandatory decision on your part. You can do as you wish and remain shallow of spirit and of life, or you can live a life doing for others first. The more you care for others, your spirit deepens and is strengthened with God. The end result is an iron-clad bond with the Lord.

When you were a child in your learning years, God planted this seed of love deep within your soul. God provides you with parents who will hopefully encourage you to be kind, gentle, and care for others with love. Just as you learn of God and grow to love Him more each day, you become an example of this feeling and this gentleness and calmness, flowing to others, never expecting any kind of reward for sharing your way of life. As the years slowly pass, your devotion to God and trusting faith, enables this small seed to grow. All of your reactions to others are determined by what your heart tells you to do, as God lives within your heart.

I once saw a picture of an iceberg in the water. You only see a small portion of it floating on the water, but underneath the water is the true size. It is of immense proportion. The seed of a person starts off small like the upper part of the iceberg. Then years pass, the depth of your spirit grows gigantic with much strength, just as the unseen part of the iceberg mass is veiled by the deep waters of the ocean.

Learn of Me and I will give you peace and all understanding.

THE VOID

Cessation of a loved one's life often brings division between the remaining family and friends. Without that person, it may seem you no longer have that comfortable footpath to reach each other in your deepest time of need. The passage that had existed in and through that person is gone, no matter how great the remaining need. Your sorrow is intensified by the deep void that remains within your heart. You are trapped and have no place to go to escape the pain that won't disappear from your life. There is no truce between you and this lonely journey which you must complete alone. Many times fear, despair, and a sense of desertion enter the portal of your spirit, continually whispering deceptive emotions and sensations, binding you until you feel you will never succeed in overcoming this ever-present loss.

The emptiness of what no longer exists can truly overtake you, leaving you severely downtrodden in your broken life. Death is a diseased demon, trying to destroy all families and dear friends. Yes, death is a journey all must take. But it can surely leave the ones left behind disillusioned, often struggling to fend for themselves, unprepared without the loved one that has passed away. Moments of laughter and talking, on all sorts of subjects, suddenly cease with that special person.

We must have enormous faith in God to overcome this tragedy and to know in your spirit that it is not the end. Truthfully, it is the beginning of a new and better life, for both them and us. We can be together again with the ones we love, to live together forever.

Remember, the Lord is always standing beside you. He is holding your hand, making it possible for your soul to glide through this, without grief, but with loving, total acceptance of things to come. The Lord is always gentle with you, telling you it will be okay. He is with you through all life's difficulties. Let Him fill the empty void that you carry.

By Chris Linnebur

WHISPERING WINDS OF THE DEPARTED

You never know from which direction death may come, in the whispering winds of your precious life. It may come from the direction that you caused all by yourself. You may no longer care for the life that was freely given to you as a gift from God. You no longer desire the will to live. In your mind all is pointless and hopeless. There is an empty space in your heart where love used to live. Sometime ago, without warning, love departed from your life. Much of your time is spent searching for a way to fill the empty space, but to no avail. The end result is still that empty place where love used to live. Your direction no longer exists. Your life has lost its glory and you choose not to care for yourself any longer. In your heart and mind, death would be your way out. All your dreams and wishes are totally saturated by the taste of death.

There is another unknown direction in which death may come. It may come as a sudden surprise. A surprise is normally pleasant and a feast to indulge yourself in. But, this is not that kind of surprise. It is an act of deceitfulness beyond all reasoning. This deed is done by a stranger performing a senseless act with no mercy or reason. Your precious life is stolen from you in an instant. Your right to choose your direction in life is snuffed out rapidly, just like blowing out a flame on a candle. And there is no turning back, the only available path is this act of violence which came upon you. Your soul will forever search for peace but you will never be able to find it.

Your direction to death could turn out to be purely accidental. You can be doing fine and in the best of health. You are at the top of your world and along comes a freak accident. You have no control over it; there are no warning flares, just an end to your perfect world.

104

Your death could come to you as naturally as birth. You may linger, being well aware of your final outcome. This delay may be a blessing in disguise, being allowed to get your life in order and making your peace with God if you had not done already done so.

No matter which direction that day comes from, each day of your life should be lived as a swan's song, your farewell appearance. Sing your song of life as beautifully as you can, with all your might and breath. Each day should be precious. Fix your eyes and your heart in the Lord's direction. He will fill all the empty spaces of your life. The Lord will give you the ability to forgive when there is no forgiveness. He will give you the strength needed to endure all aspects of your life. Raise up your hands, praising the Lord, for you never know when the whispering winds of the departed will come and stand upon your doorstep.

By Sharon Teal Coray

SHOES OF DESPAIR

Has there been a time in your life when all was well with you? You had accomplished much after many years of hard work. The elegant riches of this world were not in order for you, but you were content with all you had. Then you were to receive the reward of all times, the golden ring was coming within your grasp. You are filled with joy beyond comprehension, your dreams and hopes of having a home of your own came true – a gift from the heart of God.

It was your gold mine. You were stepping up to a life of security, truly enjoying the sweet smell of the wildflowers and roses in your own yard, sitting peacefully on your swing with the cool evening air touching your face. Watching the leaves on your trees swaying ever so gently in the breeze, you take in what a time of wonder and joy present in these miraculous days. Just as God made it possible for you to have a beautiful first home, man can step in and destroy your moment of happiness, without emotion or concern of your well-being. Within a flash, all of your glory and reward can be taken away from you. You now wear the shoes of despair.

What a weary path you must now follow. There are no more hopes and dreams. All was lost by a trusted friend. You were not young when this tragedy happened in your life. Your body was of an oldster, with a fragile frame due to years of working. It was impossible to regain your footing with this shattering burden now placed on your shoulders. Your path in life was forever changed and you were lost.

Your tears beckoned for the Lord's help, as you can do nothing to correct this wrong done to you. No longer will you wear the good garments of days gone by. On your feet are the shoes you will wear until the end of time – those of despair. Your only contentment is trusting in the Lord. You will forever live in seclusion, a daily sojourner with the Lord, in order to just survive.

This will be the greatest test of all trials for you. You trust that the Lord will provide for all your needs, just as your Father in Heaven takes care of all homeless creations in this world. Your life has forever changed and there is no turning back. You can only go forward into days of an unknown future. Your desires will only be to survive. Your hopes are that the Lord hears and answers your prayers. Your new home will be what the Lord provides. The earthly riches are forever gone. But you realize it is better to live an obedient, humble life with the Lord, than live otherwise, forgetting why you are truly here.

The stars are still within your reach. The light they put forth is for other possibilities now. The road will be harder than you have ever experienced, but the Lord will see you through. Just as you wear the shoes of despair, the Lord will too – which means, as long as you choose to live in despair, the Lord will stay by you and bring you out of it. Always remember whatever your circumstances, God is right there with you in those circumstances. He wears what you wear. He goes where you go. His compassion is real. He loves you and His greatest desire is for you to trust him so He can bring you out of the adverse circumstances. Let him shower you with all His grace, and let Him give you all the strength you need to come through it and out of it.

MAY I CARRY YOUR HOLLOW SOUL?

Is your heart being consumed by suffering or is it merely the question of a hollow soul? At times, you feel the emptiness is more agonizing than a simple affliction to you. Hours and then days pass, with no love or attentiveness, required for a soul to live. It feels like a vast aperture, forever swallowing up and overwhelming your being. The memories of the past seem too far off in the distance to touch, and each new day carries the same emptiness. What is the sense of going on if no one cares? To be alone and not cared for is the crime of all time. It can destroy you without any warning. My spirit has gone through this hollowness and now it knows what to expect.

My spirit survived and is still strong. I wish to be there for another so that I can help them survive this crime brought upon them. Place this transgression on me so my heart can bear your sorrow, releasing you from ultimate doom. You can live again, and I will carry the emptiness on my shoulders you now bear. Jesus asks, "May I carry your hollow soul?"

Grand-daughter, Abigail Linnebur, Age 2

UNBORN CHILD

Where are you going my little unborn child? Will you inherit a life of much ease, with no strain on your part to exist, or will you enter into a life of poverty and crime. Will you have to struggle to survive all your life? One thing I must pray is for this precious unborn child to be placed in a home with all the love and care that is possible.

May your life be enriched by knowing the difference between good and evil. May your heart be constantly filled with love towards others. Live your life being kind and gentle always. May you forever be surrounded by parents and individuals who will love you, just as they love the Lord. May you be named just as a beautiful queen receives her name, with much love, honor and joy. May your life make a difference in others.

May your path be guided by the hand of the Lord. God bless your coming into this world.

DREAM STORIES

"...I will pour out my spirit upon all flesh; and your sons and your daughters shall prophesy, your old men shall dream dreams, your young men shall see visions."

Joel 2:28

℞
✝

THE BURNING BUILDING

A young lady by the name of Annabe decided that it was such a beautiful day outside that she would go for a nice walk. Her direction of choice took her towards her old junior high school of long ago. As she approached the enclosed courtyard surrounding the old school she noticed that the old school was no longer in use, it was now known to many in the neighborhood as a retirement home for older people.

Annabe noticed that there were onlookers at the corner across the street from the school. There used to be a grocery store there in the now vacant building. The onlookers were looking at the school courtyard in awe, so Annabe turned her head and noticed an orange blaze surrounded by a dark mist commencing from the cellar windows of the school. Her only thought was to enter the building with great haste and try to get the inhabitants out as soon as possible, hoping that no one was injured by the fire.

As Annabe approached the entrance she shouted at the onlookers across the corner for some help and they refused. Their interest was to watch the inferno reach its destructive peak without any concern about the older people in the building. So, with the corner street ogles' indifference, Annabe headed into the main entrance of the building. As she entered, many people were startled and perplexed. They were wandering aimlessly throughout the stairways and halls not knowing what to do. Annabe led each person gently from where they were to the clear air of the courtyard. This angel of true compassion worked endlessly as the halls and stairways were clear. She then proceeded to go to each separate room in the building, scurrying from floor to floor, checking for any lodgers in this massive burning building and leading them to safety. If anyone was unable to walk, she carried them out, never giving her own safety a second thought. She only wanted to help others to get out first. Annabe came upon a woman at the top of the stairway leaning against the corner wall. Annabe was on her way to the top floor to make her final sweep. As the two ladies' eyes met, Annabe noticed that this woman was covered in sores and wanted to be left there to die. Everyone that has passed this woman did not want to help her down the stairway as they did not want to touch her. They feared the sores would contaminate their bodies. Annabe would not hear of that. She picked up the woman in her arms and carried her to the safety of the courtyard. As they both reached the outside entrance of the building, Annabe put the woman down. In doing so, her shawl dropped from her face, revealing clear and radiant skin. All the sores were gone. The woman opened her cloak, revealing she also had a child hidden inside with her also. If it hadn't been for Annabe, the woman and her child would most certainly have perished in the fire.

As this devoted angel of a lady, Annabe, finished her rounds of the building, she continued on to the final floor. There was only one room left to check. As Annabe knocked on the door, it opened mysteriously with no one standing beside it. Annabe then noticed twelve men dressed in white robes sitting at a long wooden table in the room. She proceeded to tell them about the fire in the building and she wanted to save them from harm. They told her that all would be well and then they rewarded her with two crystal vases. On the front of the vases, roses were etched on each. The men told her again that all would be fine. After the second affirmation, the twelve men vanished from her sight. All that remained in the room was a white mist with the lingering smell of roses. Being bewildered by the occurrence, Annabe was not sure if it was real or not. But she looked down and realized she was holding the two vases in her arms, proving to her it was not a hallucination caused by the stress of her ordeal.

She then entered the hallway and noticed one more person left there, but this last individual had no lower limbs. Knowing that she had to make a quick decision on either carrying the vases out or carrying this man to safety, she chose to set down her beautiful prize. As the two exited the building, Annabe noticed all the people standing in the courtyard. Suddenly, she felt profoundly humbled, knowing she had rescued such a multitude of people. Never once thinking about herself, she was focused on just getting everyone out to safety. Annabe placed the last person down and he was no longer an invalid with no lower limbs. He stood tall and strong beside her. Behind his back he brought his arms forward and handed her to the two vases. As she carried this man out to safety, he carried her vases out to safety for her.

This beautiful angel of God could not hold back the tears of love and joy, for now she knew her path in life was to care for others and all would be blessed in her life. The miracles she witnessed were another message from God telling her of the healing abilities He had given to her for her obedience to Him. The two vases were not only gifts to her, but they represented her two gifts in life. One to care for others and one to heal others. All for the goodness that is in God's glory.

THE CHAINED WOLF

It was a crisp winter morning and my undertaking for the day was to explore an old abandoned house that was lodged in the nearby forest. Little did I know that my fun day was to be more important, far beyond my dreams and adventurous curiosity. Once in the house, I realized that I had to climb to the top story of this condemned shelter as it was the only part of the house that had something resembling a floor. The rest of the house was in a terrible state of shambles and quite dilapidated. I had not considered that this home in the forest was in such dire need of repair. It must have been abandoned for a long time.

I finally made it up to the attic, and to my amazement, the floor was made out of pieces of bedroom furniture, which still made this a dangerous experience. You had to walk on certain boards, or one wrong step and you would find yourself falling straight to the basement and maybe lying flat on your back, never to get up again. With much precise caution, I finally made it over the opposite side of the room. To my amazement, there was a large picture window at this particular end of the attic. It was as large as one entire wall. It surely was a sight to behold.

The attic on this end was level with the hill alongside the house. As I looked out at this enormous view, I could see the forest behind the house. It made me feel like I was Alice in Wonderland, looking through the glass mirror at another world. This room must have been the most beautiful room in the entire house in its day of glory. As I viewed the beauty of the winter snow on the ground, I noticed a deer approaching the glass window. Then a squirrel scurried past the deer. Then I focused on the beauty of a rabbit sitting on an old tree stump.

All of a sudden, there appeared from the dense forest, moving towards me, an enormous wolf. Once the wolf approached the glass window, he sat down. As I looked at this marvel of nature, I noticed that his chest was a white as the newly-fallen snow on the ground. He had black leopard spots mixed in with the white color on his chest. The rest of his body was jet black. It truly was an animal of great beauty and power. The wolf was unable to come any closer because he was tethered to a long tow chain. The people who lived here must have abandoned him too, just as they had deserted the house. The wolf's chain was dreadfully mangled with an accumulation of old wood, dead leaves, mixed with wet dirt frozen together from the frigid snow.

I could not help but think that this ferocious but precious animal had to carry some form of resentment having been in bondage for so long, burdened by this heavy chain. His memories of freedom were probably only an illusion. To be free again was not an option in his mind any longer. I knew that I had to go outside to try somehow to help this wondrous wolf to be free again. If he was to remain in bondage much longer, he would surely die. So I travelled down from the attic to the wooded area outside that I had viewed from the picture window. I cautiously approached the bound wolf. I tried not to show my fear of his wild nature, but I was truly apprehensive about the situation. I just decided to talk my way through the problem. I could see that the wolf felt that I would not harm him so I was able at this point to struggle with the chain to free him. It seemed like I worked on the chain for hours, but eventually I was able to free him.

I found a new friend that day. He was now free to live a new life. His choice was to come and go as he wished, but we remained devoted to each other for many years to come. The bondage was broken and I was chosen to help in this blessed event. My life was forever changed by this act of love to free a creature of God. I am glad that my adventure turned out to be much more important than just an adventure to pass a snowy afternoon.

THE ROSARIES OF THE WOODEN FLOOR

There was a tender elderly woman by the name of Maria who loved to do for others. She lived alone in a small home that her husband purchased for them so many years ago. With her husband's passing away, Maria's life was severely battered and worn down by this world; but with each new day that she awakened, she gave thanks to God with a glad heart for all she was given. Even though life was difficult and hard for Maria, she did not let her problems affect her love for others. Whenever someone was in need, she was eager to help them and her spirit was very humbled by their asking.

One day, this angel on earth was visiting her dear friend, Elizabeth. They had known each other for many years. Not one day would pass without them seeing each other. Elizabeth was in very poor health and was not expected to live much longer. As the two ladies sat a while and talked of the old days, Elizabeth mustered the strength to get off her chair and proceeded to get down on her hands and knees to clean her floor. It was the last chore of the day for her, a job that could not be neglected. Maria, noticing that her friend was much too sick to do the task that day, asked Elizabeth if she could help. The request was greatly appreciated and Maria gently helped Elizabeth rise up from the floor.

Elizabeth, now resting in a comfortable chair, continued her conversation of the olden days. Maria now had changed places with Elizabeth, and was on her knees preparing to clean the floor. Maria had an old apron on and in one of the pockets was an old scrub brush. It was a brush that her mother had given her long ago. The bristles of the brush were worn down, just like the life of this beautiful lady. On one corner of the brush handle was a carving of a heart. This engraving was put on the brush by her mother as a remembrance of the love they shared together.

With much love in her heart, Maria scrubbed the floor and listened to Elizabeth's stories. As the brush moved from one end of the floor to the other end, Maria noticed that the old dirty floor had a beautiful pattern. Amazingly, the pattern was identical to the floor she had cleaned as a child for her mother. It was of the deepest midnight blue with an array of many flowers. There was a section of the linoleum that was badly torn and no repair job could fix it. Maria proceeded to raise up the torn linoleum and to her surprise there was an old wooden floor beneath. Maria then had a thought that if she lifted up all the linoleum, she could scrub and wax the old wooden floor, and it would be more beautiful than the old torn linoleum. With her eagerness, Maria asked Elizabeth if she would agree, and the reply was yes, that would be wonderful.

As Maria slowly removed the linoleum, there was a layer of newspapers covering the wooden floor which had to be removed first before she could clean. Then she noticed a slightly deeper portion of the floor. It was quite a large indentation, so Maria put her hand in the floor to clean it out. As she pulled her hand out, there were three rosaries interwoven between her fingers. At that moment, when she saw the rosaries, her spirit was touched by another Divine spirit and He talked to her.

The spirit told her of her life, past and present. He told her that the old linoleum floor that she tried to clean was the representation of her old life as a child, and her mother was the foundation. The old wooden floor that she wanted to scrub and shine because it was so worn and battered was her life now. The rosaries represented her honor and love to God. She was told to pray to God daily and He would make her life better.

Just as the floor was to be renewed, God would renew her life again. Her spirit will also be as beautiful as the heavens. This was God's reward to this beautiful lady who loved others more than herself. She would be renewed in spirit which would give her the strength to go on for many years to come. Her burden would no longer be heavy. It would be on God's shoulders instead. Her burden while on earth would be as light as angels' wings.

THE WHITE LAMB

It was a cold, discouraging, winter day. The trees were bare and the land was blanketed with newly-fallen, fresh snow. In the middle of the field was a large brick building which served as a school campus for many children. All the students were close friends and they all had one way of thinking. They despised anyone that had any good in them. Within the walls of this campus there lived one young girl who was not part of the main group. This was her first year at this school. She was alone and was considered different from the rest of the students. None of the other students liked this young lady and always devoted their free time trying to figure out new ways to mock and torment her. She was their prime target daily for this favorite past-time.

Although they would not admit it, there was something special about this girl that made the other students jealous of her. They twisted it into always wanting to harm her. Although she was truly alone, she had contentment knowing the Lord. She would spend hours praying and singing. This brought her great joy and comfort.

One morning, this precious girl was walking on the school grounds. She walked across the white frozen earth beneath her feet and kept a steady course towards the tree with the bare tree limbs. She tried several times to reach up to touch the bare limbs, but she was too short to do so. She continued to walk further, crossing over a hill not too far from the school. Her mind was troubled by the thoughts of how much she was hated by the other girls and that she had no friends. She knew that she was different from the other children. Her desire towards others was always to be kind to them, never to harm any of them. But her kindness at the school was refused and she was marked as an outsider. As she pondered these thoughts, she passed over another small hill. She stopped for a few moments to admire the beautiful scenery when suddenly, out of nowhere, there appeared a white lamb. He was a very young lamb and had a loving essence about him. Drawing closer, when the young girl looked at the lamb, he just leaped into her arms. The lamb seemed to smile at her as he glanced into her eyes. A strange feeling came over the girl. It was as if they knew each other from long ago. She held this lamb ever so tightly in her arms and rejoiced on and on. She finally had a friend to be with her. They played together and she laughed for many hours. There was no sorrow overshadowing their time together.

Just as twilight set in across the sky, darkness crept towards them, coming up the hill. The darkness grew and as it came closer, it took on the shape of the children coming towards them. They had seen the young girl and the lamb playing together. Their only thought was to destroy the girl and kill the lamb. As the children came closer, they began picking up rocks to use as weapons. They each carried as many rocks as their little hands could hold. Once in position, the children started to throw these rocks at the little girl and her lamb. The girl saw the danger coming and her only thought was to protect the lamb. The lamb represented the hope and goodness in this world to her, and she was going to stop them from destroying the lamb. With protective reflexes, she placed the precious lamb on some soft ground and then lay over the lamb to shield him from any harm. As the attackers came closer, the rocks began to strike her with greater force until her little body finally lay limp and lifeless.

As the callous children laughed at their triumph, an amazing thing happened before their eyes, causing them to instantly drop the rocks remaining in their hands. They all fell to their knees in fear. Yes, they won their victory in killing their enemy, the little girl, but they became witness to seeing the spirit of the little girl and the lamb departing. DID THEY KILL THE LAMB ALSO? As they watched, the lamb changed into a man, dressed in a white robe, carrying the little girl in his arms, and she was now the lamb. The man was Jesus, and he was taking the little girl away from this cruel and senseless world. She will now always be sheltered by Jesus, just as she protected the white lamb from harm.

HOME WORK

"To everything there is a season, and a time to every purpose under heaven: A time to be born, and a time to die; a time to plant, and a time to pluck up that which is planted; a time to kill, and a time to heal; a time to break down, and a time to build up."

Ecclesiastes 3: 1-3

℞
†

"Alaska Homestead" by Chris Linnebur

HOMESTEADING IN ALASKA
(A biography of David Linnebur)

The following notice was readily available for the public to read –"Land Management of the U.S. Government is allowing open homesteading in Alaska. Anyone interested, contact the Bureau of Land Management." The requirements listed were: 21 years old, 160 acres per family, the individual filing was to select the land they wanted and stake out their homestead.

The rules were very clear. Within 3 years, the individual or family had to clear 20 acres of land and that portion of land had to be cultivated. There must be a one-room house built on the property with one door, one window, and an outhouse constructed 50 feet away from the house. At the end of three years, after all requirements were met, you could obtain the title to the property at the cost of $3.00 per un-cleared acre. The criteria listed above were only the minimum rules that must be met. If the family wanted to do more, clear more acres, build a larger home, they could.

In the spring of 1959, I was 12 years old, and my father read about the Homesteading Act available in Alaska. We were living in Palmer, Alaska, at the time. The notice was not limited to Alaska only. It was nationwide. The Bureau of Land Management was making available to the public, homesteading land of 120 to 160 acre parcels. You were required to select a parcel of your own choice and mark it personally, then take the information to the BLM and file on that specific property. Upon filing for the property, if there were no disputes against your claim, you would be issued an interim title, which would not allow anyone else to file on your property for three years.

Our family received our interim title in March, 1959.

My dad, mother, three sisters, and I continued to live in Palmer and go out to the homestead on weekends, which was 42 miles away in the wilderness. Driving down a snow-covered, single-lane, dirt road, we began clearing a road, a third of a mile long, into the woods where we would build our home. It took the entire month of March to clear the road and an area about 100 square feet where the house would sit. To accomplish this, we had to shovel approximately eight feet of snow on top of the frozen ground so we could begin to clear the trees from the road and home-site.

About mid-April, we started hauling lumber to begin building our new home. The measurements were to be 30 feet by 50 feet. The family voted on a ranch style plan with three bedrooms. There was no electricity, so all the work had to be done with hand tools. We did not have running water or a phone and the nearest conveniences were 12 miles away. Most of the work was accomplished by my father and me. We stayed in a tent during the construction, although winter lasted through April and May. The temperature could get down to zero degrees, and at times, down to -10 degrees at night, only to warm up to the 40's during the day. By the end of May, the house was ready for us to move into. Since there were no modern amenities, we built an outhouse 75 feet from the back of the house. There was a small stream about 750 feet from the house, which required going down two small hills, or steps as we called them, to reach the stream. The hills were actually 20 to 30-foot drops from the level our house was on. That is where we got our water supply for drinking, cooking, and bathing. Water had to be hauled daily for the needs of our family and livestock, consisting of cows, chickens and pigs. We hauled the water in 5-gallon buckets.

The first summer, we cleared 5 acres by hand. Our land was mainly a virgin timber stand, which had never been cleared before. There were many birch, spruce, pine, and cottonwood trees on our land. We used a double-bladed axe to chop the trees down, and used the logs for firewood. My father bought a farm tractor, which we used to pull out the tree stumps. We planted only a small garden the first summer because of all the other work that had to be done before winter set in. We built a pole barn, approximately twenty by 30 feet, out of the smaller pine trees we cut down. The pole barn was needed for our livestock to protect them from the harsh winter to come.

The stream that ran through our property was an artisan spring, which is an underground watershed that made its way to the surface. It was located 1/2 mile from our house and, since moving water does not freeze, the year-round temperature of the water was 20 degrees. We used the stream as our refrigerator. The game killed by my dad and me on hunting trips was cut up and put in plastic storage bags. We placed the bags into a wooden box and lowered the wooden boxes into the stream. We only kept a supply of meat in the stream for 3 to 5 days at a time. Since my father worked in Palmer where the bulk of the meat was stored, he would bring fresh meat to the homestead on a regular basis.

Our flour, sugar and canned vegetables were bought at the store. In Alaska, you cannot grow all the vegetables you might want. The growing season is short and you are very limited by what vegetables will grow there. There were many wild berries on the property, including strawberries, blueberries, raspberries, and cranberries. My mother made quite a few treats for us with the wild berries. During the summer months, electricity for lighting our home, if it had been available, would not have been necessary since the sun stays up 24 hours a day. We had a small portable generator which was used on Saturdays only for washing and ironing. We were grateful for the long summer days, as much work had to be accomplished before the long winter season came again.

In September, school started again. I was in the 7th grade at that time. The school my sisters and I attended was 18 miles away. Due to the remoteness of where we lived, the bus route covered a range of 40 miles. We caught the bus at 6:30 a.m. since we were on the end of the route and we were the first ones picked up. School started at 8:15 a.m. and we got out at 3:15 p.m., but didn't arrive home until 5:00 p.m. Due to the fact that my father worked rotating shifts, most mornings, I was up by 5:00 a.m. My schedule was to feed the animals for the day. I would eat a quick breakfast, get dressed, and head out for school. It was 1/3 of a mile walk to the main road from our house to catch the bus. It was a new adventure almost every day, and my 3 sisters and I had to watch out for moose and bear. During the summer, we received numerous visits from the local animal population, so we knew we had to watch for them and be very cautious. Sometimes we would have to walk as much as an extra 1/4 mile to get around the animals – it was their home too. In Alaska, the snow in winter can be very deep and the temperatures very cold. Temperatures from -40 to -60 degrees below zero were normal. Snow from 2 to 3 feet was normal. Life does not stop; you just adapt and adjust.

It was typically dark except for 4 to 6 hours of daylight every day from the first of October until the end of March. When you live in the city, or even in a small town like Palmer of 700 people, you don't experience the darkness like you do in a remote area. The Northern Lights are more brilliant in the wilderness and the skies are crystal clear at night, stretching infinitely. Our first winter, we had to kill many wolves and a few moose that came into our yard. The moose had to be killed because they tend to follow a path to the end, never turning around, and our path ended at our back door. The wolves on the other hand, were trying to get at our livestock.

Again, we did not have electricity or running water, so our lighting needs to do homework was supplied by oil lamps. They were similar to the scented lamps used today, except we used kerosene. When there was a lot of snow on the ground, we would bring in washtubs full of snow and melt it down for our water usage. Due to the cold temperatures during the winter months, we no longer used the stream for our refrigerator. We had a mud room attached to the house which was not heated. We kept our food requiring refrigeration there, along with our winter gear. We used 30 cords of wood to heat the house and barn each winter. A cord of wood is a stack 4 feet wide, 4 feet high, and 8 feet deep. The fires had to burn 24 hours a day. We used barrel stoves for heating, which is a 55-gallon oil drum laid on its side, lined with fire brick. It was a very efficient heating system and the wood was plentiful.

In early spring, my father made arrangements with a logging company to buy the birch trees we planned to clear that summer on an additional 10 acres of our land. Part of that agreement allowed us to use their heavy equipment to clear the land. It would have taken us 3 months to clear by hand what it took only 5 days to clear with the equipment. The second summer, we planted 10 acres. 5 of those acres were planted in oats and peas, and the other 5 in brome grass, used for pasture. Regarding our livestock, there was not much call for bull calves since most cattle farmers were in the dairy business. Rather than immediately killing the bull calves, we made an arrangement with the dairy farmers to pick them up and raise them, giving them a percentage of the profits when butchered for veal.

The second summer was occupied by taking care of the expanded beef herd and building a second chicken coop and pigpen. Due to the increased cleared acreage, the wild animal population on our land diminished somewhat. The second summer also marked the arrival of the squatters. Squatters were people who settled on public land with a hope to acquire a title. As I stated earlier, when my father filed on the land, a temporary title was issued, all part of the rules and requirements of getting a clear title. If you did not meet all the requirements before the three years were up, someone could file a cross claim on the same property and file for a temporary entitlement. The exception to this agreement was the clause that stated, "A squatter could move on to the property, build a one-room house and claim no more than 10 acres maximum". This is what happened to us. We could not force the squatters to get off the property and he was given a clear title to the 10 acres he claimed. Also, during that second summer, we started clearing another 10 acres so that the following year we would be able to get our final title to our remaining acres. That summer of 1960 brought many more homesteaders from the lower states. Bringing their families meant a new school would be started in Willow, which was closer to my home. The school consisted of three Quonset huts. They were approximately 30 by 60 feet each, housing grades 1 through 8. The hour and a half bus ride was reduced to only 1/2 hour. Our classroom was a combination of the 6th, 7th, and 8th grades.

The winter passed, as usual, with cold temperatures and lots of snow. Some of our time was spent that winter cutting pine logs into usable lumber, to make kitchen cabinets, a breakfast bar and paneling for our dining room. We also completely wired the house for electricity and put in plumbing so the house would be ready when we got electricity sometime in the future.

Early in the spring of 1961, we hired a bulldozer to completely clear the last of our acreage, in order to receive final title to our property. We received our final deed in July, after $275.00 for the 85 un-cleared acres of land was paid to the BLM. Over the next 4 years, we became sharecroppers with the other homesteaders around us who did not have farm equipment. Every spring I would plant their fields and in the fall, I would harvest their grain crop, keeping 20 percent for us. I left home in June of 1965, and my father stopped farming. From 1961 to 1973, my father worked in heavy construction.

As I reflect back on the way of life prior to us homesteading, I lived like any city-raised child. I was a typical 12-year-old adolescent when I moved to the wilderness, but I had to mature rapidly. When there was spare time, I would wander through the woods, on foot with my dog, following bear tracks or other animal trails. I had numerous encounters with wildlife. I knew where the wolf dens were and where to find mink and wolverine. I learned to respect the animals that shared our land. To this day, I find it very disdainful to take another life unnecessarily, whether man or animal. I learned to stand alone at a young age, making decisions normally not required until the late teens. I learned how to exist with only what is provided by nature or by hard work.

David Linnebur, 7 years old,
Georgie's Husband

I HAVE NOT FORGOTTEN YOU- WELCOME TO HEAVEN

"For so an entrance shall be ministered unto you abundantly into the everlasting kingdom of our Lord and Saviour Jesus Christ."

II Peter 1:11

Georgie's Mother, Mercedes Zdunowski,
and Tezra

IT IS TOO LATE!

The door was opened but now it is shut.
The passage way to your life, and all your
miraculous memories have been trapped
forever in a non-existent world. No one knows
how to restore what has been lost. This
precious life has been altered forever. All the
joys and moments that have been shared over
many years have fused with the mind, never to
be re-visited again.

The sorrow for all involved is more than
anyone can face. In your life there were
wonderful lessons learned, given to you by
guardians and wise elders, happy memories
filled with joy and laughter. Love, without end,
reigned supreme in your life.

Then came the shadow, a question rising and taking form. Did all these things really happen, or was it just a dream? Did I really exist or was I even here? There are no more songs to be sung or movies to be watched, just living in a strange world that makes no sense. Communication has no foothold or place through the intrinsic passage way of your body. The once scholarly mind, which spoke multitudes of languages, is forever buried in the abyss of the soul, never to rise again.

At times, a far distant thought comes in clear. The next moment, it leaves no trace of its form, leaving you with the illusion of madness. As the thought becomes more and more distant, becoming totally out of reach, anger sets in, wild searching action and thoughts go crazy. You are left feeling your mind is on a carousel to nowhere.

You try to hold on to all those who are close and dear to your heart, but one by one, the torrid winds carry them off to a place you have never been before. Words, at this point, have no meaning. Time is unimportant. Days are at a standstill. Your mind drifts like the sands on the beautiful beach you once walked upon. Old memories become crystal clear from time to time, while newer memories and loved ones are a struggle to see and relate to.

What is this terrible disease that struck my mother who was still the shining star of my life? I still have the memory of our life together, but she has a different path now. It is too late to regain our early lives together. But I will always be there in a spirit-to-spirit connection with her.

There is a chair next to her bed, in her room that seems so empty, but it is not. I sent my best friend to take my place with her. He sits in that chair and never leaves her side, holding her close to Him, trying to console her. He gives her all the peace she needs. Covering her with the blanket of His glory, and surrounding her being with His powerful grace, He spiritually puts back all the broken pieces of her life so she can live again. Mami's liberation is in the Lord's hands now. Only He can restore what has been taken away from her by this harsh world, the worst way of deception known to man – Alzheimer's

Mami has passed away now and the Lord was there to walk her into His Kingdom. There is no more pain and no more tears, just the sweet life with the Lord. Family and dear friends who had gone ahead are all together now, at peace, worshipping the Lord.

I truly look forward to the day I will be able to see my precious and beloved Mami again. This time it will not be too late and we will be together forever.

About Georgianna Linnebur

Georgie, Salt Lake City, 2014

Georgie Linnebur lives in Salt Lake City, but has travelled and lived all around the United States. She started writing as a young lady, and over the years, God has encouraged her by "downloading" to her, many inspirational conversations and stories.

The stories compiled in this book, were given to her from the Lord, to give her hope and encouragement for her current situation. Now, Georgie wishes to share these stories with you that you may also realize that the Lord is always alongside of you, and wants to reveal His great love for you. He is there to help you, answer every prayer, and show you how to love others.

As you read these stories, may you be blessed and encouraged, that with Georgie, you too can say, "I survived, and now I thrive".

The Author, Georgianna Linnebur,
32 years old, in Lexington Park, Maryland

27 years old

40th Birthday

Georgie, Salt Lake City Cemetery, 2013

Psalm 91

He that dwelleth in the secret place of the Most High shall abide under the shadow of the Almighty.

I will say of the Lord, He is my refuge and my fortress: my God; in Him will I trust.

Surely he shall deliver thee from the snare of the fowler, and from the noisome pestilence.

He shall cover thee with his feathers, and under his wings shalt thou trust: his truth shall be thy shield and buckler.

Thou shalt not be afraid for the terror by night; nor for the arrow that flieth by day; nor for the pestilence that walketh in darkness; nor for the destruction that wasteth at noonday.

A thousand shall fall at thy side, and ten thousand at thy right hand; but it shall not come nigh thee.

Only with thine eyes shalt thou behold and see the reward of the wicked.

Because thou hast made the Lord, which is my refuge, even the Most High, thy habitation; there shall no evil befall thee, neither shall any plague come nigh thy dwelling.

For he shall give his angels charge over thee, to keep thee in all thy ways. They shall bear thee up in their hands, lest thou dash thy foot against a stone.

Thou shalt tread upon the lion and adder: the young lion and the dragon shalt thou trample under feet.

Because he hath set his love upon me, therefore, will I deliver him; I will set him on high, because he hath known my name.

He shall call upon me, and I will answer him: I will be with him in trouble; I will deliver him, and honor him.

With long life will I satisfy him, and show him my salvation.

www.ingramcontent.com/pod-product-compliance
Lightning Source LLC
LaVergne TN
LVHW021452080426
835509LV00018B/2251